Langley's Aero Engine of 1903

Charles M. Manly standing in the aviator's car of the partially assembled Langley Aerodrome A working on its engine. The Aerodrome is poised on its catapult mounted on a specially designed houseboat located in the vicinity of Quantico, Virginia, sometime during September 1903. Now on exhibit at the Smithsonian Institution. (Smithsonian photo A18804.)

Langley's Aero Engine of 1903

Edited by

Robert B. Meyer, Jr.

SMITHSONIAN INSTITUTION PRESS

City of Washington • 1971

UNITED STATES GOVERNMENT PRINTING OFFICE
WASHINGTON : 1971

Prologue

How many things by season seasoned are
to their right praise and true perfection!

The Merchant of Venice, Act V, Scene 1

At the turn of the century, those who dealt seriously with experiments in heavier-than-air "flying machines" were regarded as an eccentric fringe element, subject to derision by both the general public and the press. Thus, it took an extra amount of moral courage and conviction for prominent men to jeopardize their professional reputations by attempting to advance the state of the art. Such a man was Samuel Pierpont Langley, third Secretary of the Smithsonian Institution, whose efforts and dedication gave heart to others to also reach for the sky. However, in spite of his past accomplishments in the fields of astronomy and meteorology, Langley also could not escape the derision and ridicule of the press (Figure 1) as noted in the following skeptically flippant editorial from the *Washington Post* of 14 November 1898, regarding the second unsuccessful attempt to launch his man-carrying aerodrome.

14 November 1898
The Washington Post, Editorial Page

"WAIT FOR THE FLYING-MACHINE—We note the published statement that the authorities are seriously considering the question of airships for the army in time of war. General Greely, of the Signal Service, proposed it, we believe, and now Professor S. P. Langley, of the Smithsonian Institution, the National Museum, the National Astrophysical Observatory, and perhaps a few other government positions which we haven't time to remember at the moment, has been called in to cooperate. General Greely, so far as we know, has never yet built and operated a flying-machine, but he knows all about them, understands them perfectly, and besides has rendered illustrious public service such as trying to discover the north pole, and actually saving our army at Santiago. Professor Langley, however, is not only an expert in aerostatics, he has actually con-

v

structed an airship. He gave eight years of his time, or about that much, to the work, and at last he finished it. Furthermore, the ship really flew when tested. It flew half a mile, and, what is more, it didn't hurt anything or anybody except itself. Very likely it wouldn't have done even that if it hadn't stopped so suddenly.

"Both General Greely and Professor Langley are convinced that the practicable airship is a possibility. Of course, they don't mean a thing that will fly only half a mile, that cannot carry passengers, and that alights with too great violence. Professor Langley built that ship merely as a demonstration of his theories. He never intended it for real use. But now that the government has agreed to consider the proposition in earnest, and General Greely has given it his official sanction, and Professor Langley has promised to contribute to the project all the results of his experiments and adumbrations, the enterprise takes on a very hopeful aspect. As far as the *Post* is concerned, we are in a state of pleasurable excitement. The flying-machine has always been a favorite dream of ours. For years past we have been looking forward to a time when we should see other people flying about in airships and going from place to place without dust or heat or any other discomforts of travel. We have never taken a vivid interest in flying-machines that carried no passengers. The mere abstract demonstrations of science possess no charms for us. But an airship in which the inventor travels is our idea of a spectacular performance, and we anticipate it with an anxiety and a fervor far beyond all words.

"We are not yet in a position to state the time at which the Greely-Langley flying-machine will make its trial trip. We know only that the enterprise is in most capable and experienced hands, and we believe that, early in the next century, it will materialize. We shall do our best to be at the launching. We intend to practice longevity with most industrious enthusiasm in the meanwhile. We should never forgive ourselves were we so careless as to die before the ceremony."

Discouragement and failure haunt all pioneering efforts and Langley was no exception. After the second unsuccessful attempt alluded to in Figure 1, the machine was never launched again and when he died in 1906, Langley was convinced that his efforts had been in vain.

Author David Fairchild indicates Langley's reaction to the failure of his dreams.[1]

"Professor Langley's discouragement, after the plunge which wrecked his only large-scale machine, is reflected in an account given me by

[1] *The World Was My Garden* (New York: Charles Scribner's Sons, 1939), pp. 332–333.

vi

FigURE 1.—"The Birds Chorus: 'Wonder Which of Us Was the Model!'" *The Evening Star*, Washington, D.C., 9 December 1903. (Smithsonian photo A4411.)

Doctor John Brashear, a noted astronomer who was for many years the best-loved citizen of Pittsburgh. Doctor Brashear said that he was in Washington shortly after the disastrous plunge into the Potomac, and Professor Langley sent word that he would like to see him. They had been very warm friends when Professor Langley was at the Allegheny Observatory in Pittsburgh.

" 'As I entered his office in the Smithsonian,' Doctor Brashear said, 'Professor Langley met me and grasped me by both hands and said, 'Brashear, I'm ruined, my life is a failure.' He took me to the desk and showed me two bits of steel. They were the two triggers which had failed to release his machine as it slid down the ways to get its start in the air. Instead they had caught and held it, with the result that the machine dived into the water.

" 'He cried like a child,' continued Doctor Brashear. 'You may not know it, but he was a very emotional man. I tried to comfort him. I reminded him of his discoveries in astrophysics, but he would not be consoled. I believe,' said Doctor Brashear, 'that he died a bitterly disappointed man.' "

Fitting recognition of Langley's aeronautical contributions came in 1908, two years after he died, when the Smithsonian Regents established the Langley Medal for Aerodromics which was awarded for significant aeronautical accomplishments. The fifth recipient of this award was Langley's "aide in aerodromics," Charles Matthews Manly on 12 December 1929. "The exceptional action was taken in recognition of the fact that the outstanding merit of Mr. Manly's invention and construction of the light, radial, gasoline airplane engine has become more and more apparent in the last years." [2]

---

[2] *Annual Report of the Smithsonian Institution, 1931*, pp. 7–8. The recipients of the Langley Medal for Aerodromics, to date, are: Wilbur and Orville Wright, 1909; Glenn H. Curtiss and Gustave Eiffel, 1913; Charles A. Lindbergh, 1927; Charles Matthews Manly (posthumously) and Richard Evelyn Byrd, 1929; Joseph Sweetman Ames, 1935; Jerome C. Hunsaker, 1955; Robert H. Goddard (posthumously), 1960; Hugh Latimer Dryden, 1962; Alan B. Shepard, Jr., 1964; Wernher von Braun, 1967.

Acknowledgments

Copies of the original manuscript were sent to Vernon W. Balzer, son of Stephen M. Balzer; John McK. Ballou, business associate of Stephen M. Balzer; Charles W. Manly, son of Charles M. Manly; and C. B. Veal, business associate of Charles M. Manly.

I am particularly grateful to Mr. Vernon Balzer for giving the National Air and Space Museum his father's papers, and to Mr. John Ballou for his biography of Stephen Balzer and his comments about the original manuscript.

I also wish to thank Mr. C. H. Gibbs-Smith, Keeper of the Public Relations Department, Victoria and Albert Museum, London, and Lt. Commander W. J. Tuck, Keeper of Aeronautical Engines, Science Museum, London, for their help in preparing the present manuscript.

Finally I take this opportunity to express my gratitude to Mr. S. Paul Johnston, Director, and Mr. Paul E. Garber, Assistant Director, Aeronautics, and Head Curator and Historian of the National Air and Space Museum for their advice and encouragement.

The material contained herein is chosen for its pertinence to the development of the Langley aero engine and to the contribution of the three principal participants in its development. Most of the correspondence is excerpted from the originals which are on file in the National Air and Space Museum, Smithsonian Institution. Since all questions pertaining to the Langley engine cannot be answered in this brief account, additional information is available to scholars at the National Air and Space Museum, Smithsonian Institution, in the form of an index of 1,000 cards referencing the Langley papers contained in this Museum. Two typewritten manuscripts are also available, which elaborate more fully on the subject discussed here, and consist of 1,200 and 600 pages, respectively.

In matters of spelling and punctuation, modern usage has been introduced only when the content was unclear or erroneous, in which case the proper terminology is supplied in brackets by the editor. Grammatical lapses have been retained except in a few cases where change of a single letter could be classed as a correction of spelling. All proper names have been corrected to conform with approved spellings or usages. Throughout Chapters 1 through 8 editorial comments are set in italics, the correspondence in roman.

Contents

		Page
Prologue	....	v
Acknowledgments	....	ix
Introduction	....	1
Chapter 1: Influence of the Balzer Automobile Engine, 1894 ..		9
Chapter 2: Influence of the De Dion-Bouton Automobile Engine, 1900	....	17
Chapter 3: Balzer-Manly Aero Engine, First Stage	....	27
Chapter 4: Balzer-Manly Aero Engine, Second Stage	....	84
Chapter 5: Balzer-Manly Aero Engine, Third Stage	....	97
Chapter 6: Balzer-Manly Aero Engine, Fourth Stage	....	104
Chapter 7: Evaluation of the Balzer-Manly Aero Engine	......	130
Chapter 8: Evaluation of Balzer's and Manly's Contributions to the Engine	....	157
Summary	....	184
Epilogue	....	188
List of Names	....	189

Introduction

With the advent of the successful application of power to heavier-than-air craft by the Wright brothers in 1903, flying became a practical reality. Although Sir George Cayley of England had developed the first man-carrying glider, fifty years earlier, it had been without power and, therefore, had had little practical value.

The genius of the Wright brothers lay in their airframe, propeller, and control developments, making the Kitty Hawk Flyer so aerodynamically efficient that it was able to carry a man in flight powered only by a 200-pound 12-horsepower engine.

A contemporary man-carrying powered airplane was developed by the Smithsonian Institution known as the Langley Aerodrome A. Being less efficient aerodynamically than the Kitty Hawk Flyer, it was abandoned after two unsuccessful launchings by catapult over the Potomac River during the last quarter of 1903. The engine, 52 horsepower and weighing 200 pounds, was of the most advanced aeronautical design in the world at the turn of the century. It has been on display in the Smithsonian Institution for the past fifty years and is known as the Balzer-Manly aero engine to distinguish it from a model engine built by the same designers.

This book presents for the first time in a comprehensive and correct manner the story of Professor Langley's magnificent aero engine or as it is otherwise known, the Balzer-Manly aero engine. For the most part the text and illustrations are from original source material not previously published. As a result, long-standing uncertainties concerning the engine are resolved for the first time. We are now able to answer such questions as: How was Manly able to double the engine's power without any design changes three weeks after he removed it from Balzer's shop and started working on it at the Smithsonian? Why did Manly change it from an air-cooled rotary radial to a water-cooled static radial? Why did the Smithsonian Institution wait twenty-five years to award Manly the Langley Medal? Why did Balzer wait for

1

thirty years to press his claim? Why did the Aviation Industry wait thirty years before adopting the basic design features of the engine?

The greatest mystery, however, was the lack of credit accorded to Balzer. It was remarked upon by Dr. C. G. Abbot, then Secretary of the Smithsonian Institution, in a letter he wrote on 26 June 1933 (now in Smithsonian Archives).

"We recognize that Manly followed Balzer's general design and used some parts and much experience that Balzer had been paid contract price for. We regret that Manly in his book did not give Balzer more credit. It would have been only fair of him to do so." [The book referred to is the "Langley Memoir On Mechanical Flight" in the *Smithsonian Contributions to Knowledge,* volume 27, number 3 (1911).]

This lack of recognition was further attested to by Orville Wright in his letter of 28 January 1942.[3]

"Several years [ago]. . . I read in the *New York Times* of October 25, 1931, a story that a Mr. Balzer, of New York, was the author of the basic designs of the motor. Smithsonian publications apparently represented these as being the work of Mr. Manly. As to the merits of the claims made on both sides I had no personal knowledge. But a year after the appearance of this story in the *New York Times,* Dr. Abbot made the following revealing and significant statement:

" 'Mr. Balzer, however, though very co-operative, after exceeding his contract time on the large engine by many months, did not succeed in producing more than 8 horsepower. His engine was fully paid for by Langley and removed to Washington. There Charles M. Manly, Langley's engineer, made certain alterations in it, whereby he raised its output to 21 horsepower. Calculations indicating that this was insufficient, Manly designed and constructed an engine on similar lines to Balzer's, but with some features from European engine practice, and some of his own invention.' "

It is important to realize that the engine would not have existed without the combined efforts of three men: Samuel Pierpont Langley who created the need, determined the specifications, and saw to it that the money was provided; Stephen Marius Balzer who designed, built, and developed the engine in its original configuration; and Charles Matthews Manly who redesigned and rebuilt the engine greatly increasing its horsepower and improving its reliability. Each man had brought to the task his unique set of qualifications.

---

[3] *The Papers of Wilbur and Orville Wright,* volume 2 (New York: McGraw-Hill Book Company, Inc., 1953), p. 1170.

FIGURE 2.—Samuel P. Langley. Photograph is a gift of Mrs. Charles W. Manly. (Smithsonian photo A512.)

SAMUEL PIERPONT LANGLEY

Born in New England, Samuel Pierpont Langley (1834–1906) be· came especially interested in astronomy and mathematics as a student

3

in various private schools. The necessity of earning a living, however, prevented his going to college. He studied civil engineering and architecture on his own and worked mainly in Chicago and St. Louis as an architect.

Returning to New England in 1864, he abandoned his profession, and spent several years building telescopes in his spare time. After a year in Europe, he joined the Harvard Observatory, and became a professor of mathematics and was in charge of the observatory at Annapolis. Shortly afterward he became professor of astronomy and physics at Western University, Pennsylvania, and Director of the Allegheny Observatory. In order to buy equipment for the Observatory he sold "accurate time" to the Pennsylvania Railroad. Twice a day the master clock in his observatory synchronized the exact time to every station on the rail lines extending for 8,000 miles.

By 1880 he had invented the bolometer, an instrument so sensitive to heat that for the first time accurate discriminations could be made between various narrow portions of the solar spectrum. It was soon adapted by astronomers and physicists for their experimental work.

In 1887 he became Secretary of the Smithsonian Institution, and before long had established an astrophysical laboratory. He is best known, however, for his aeronautical experiments. Rescuing from skepticism this subject, which has now become so important, he made careful investigations of the physics of mechanical flight. As early as 1896 he built steamdriven aircraft models of about thirteen-foot wingspan which made repeated flights of one-half to three-quarters of a mile.

STEPHEN MARIUS BALZER

Upon the death of his father in 1873, Stephen Marius Balzer (1864-1940) emigrated with his mother from Hungary to New York.

Serving an apprenticeship at Tiffany's as a watchmaker, he became a journeyman in 1883 and specialized in repairing chronometers.

The next year he left Tiffany's to work for the Davids Machine Works of New York City, later becoming its superintendent. While at Davids he studied engineering at Cooper Union night school. In 1889 he invented a counting register for which, three years later, his company was awarded the Gold Medal of Superiority by the American Institute. In 1893 a United States patent was assigned to the company covering Balzer's register. It is the most widely used of all his inventions, being found in nearly all speedometers for automobiles today.

By 1894 he had designed and built the first automobile to run in New York City. It was powered by a three-cylinder, rotary, air-cooled

FIGURE 3.—Stephen M. Balzer. Photograph is a gift of Mr. John McK. Ballou. (Smithsonian photo A49987.)

5

382-902 O - 71 - 2

FIGURE 4.—Charles M. Manly. Photograph taken by Underwood & Underwood; gift of Mrs. Basil Manly. (Smithsonian photo A50114.)

gasoline engine, which has been on exhibit in the Smithsonian Institution since the turn of the century.

That same year he left the Davids Machine Works, and concentrated on developing his inventions. One was a backing-off mandrel to be used in any lathe for machining formed milling cutters. He was issued a patent in 1895, and received the John Scott Gold Medal in 1896 from the City of Philadelphia upon the recommendation of the Franklin Institute.

In 1898 Balzer's engine-building ability came to the attention of Langley who had wisely decided that a gasoline engine would be more practical for his proposed man-carrying airplane than a steam power plant.

CHARLES MATTHEW MANLY

As a youth in Greenville, Virginia, his association with a Cornell graduate in charge of the local electrical plant determined Charles Matthew Manly (1876–1927) to become an electrical engineer.

After a year at the University of Missouri, he entered Cornell as a sophomore, and was said to have had the best preparation in mathematics ever brought to that University. Specializing in electrical and mechanical engineering, he was among the early experimenters in the transmission of high-voltage currents.

When Langley had determined to construct a man-carrying airplane, he asked Professor R. H. Thurston, Dean of the School of Engineering in Cornell, to recommend the best young engineer he knew to assist him in this undertaking. Dr. Thurston selected Manly, who was allowed to go to Washington immediately, receiving his Cornell degree of Mechanical Engineer in absentia.

As a result of Langley's driving force both Balzer and Manly overexerted themselves. The former spent twice the contract price of the engine, using up all of his working capital in a vain effort to fully develop it, and the latter permanently impaired his health while rebuilding it.

Their combined efforts, however, produced the first modern full-size aeronautical engine. In its first stage it anticipated the rotaries of the 1900s, and in its second and subsequent stages it preceded the radials of the 1920s.

Chapter 1

Influence of the Balzer Automobile Engine
1894

*I*n order to understand the significance of the Balzer Automobile *Engine of 1894 to the later development of the Langley aero engine, the difference between a rotary engine and a static radial engine should be clear. A rotary engine, (generally known as a rotary) and the static radial engine (generally known as a radial), both have cylinders arranged around a circular crankcase like the spokes of a wheel. In the former case the cylinders, pistons, and crankcase revolve around a stationary crankshaft; and in the latter case none of these elements revolve; however, the crankshaft rotates, and the pistons reciprocate.*

When run as a rotary, the cylinders and crankcase rotate about one center, and the pistons and connecting rods rotate about another center. This eccentricity, caused by the throw of the crankshaft, permits the pistons to reciprocate relative to the cylinders, but not in the absolute sense.

Since there is no absolute reciprocation all of the parts move in the same direction with a smoothness approaching that of a turbine. In a properly balanced rotary the only noticeable vibrations come from its power impulses. A good characteristic of the rotary, therefore, is its smoothness of operation. Another advantage is the flywheel effect of the rotating parts which lessens the chance of stalling. With cylinders revolving, adequate air cooling was provided both on the ground and in the air, and this eliminated bulky and heavy water-cooling systems. Additional weight was saved over inline engines by the short crankshaft and crankcase of the radial design which also resulted in a more compact engine, hence a more maneuverable airplane.

Disadvantages of the rotary engine were: limitation on revolutions per minute due to centrifugal stress, the windage losses caused by the rotating cylinders, design limitations imposed by rotation of all parts but the crankshaft, a rather strong gyroscopic effect on the airplane during turns, the necessity of frequent overhauls, high fuel and oil consumption, and excessive throwing of oil by centrifugal force thus making the airplane dirty and a fire hazard.

In spite of these disadvantages the rotary was the best possible design for the state of the art as it existed at the turn of the century. It was produced in quantity through World War I, and powered many fighter planes.

The automobile went on exhibit at the Smithsonian Institution on 12 January 1899. It is presently displayed in the Automobile Hall of the National Museum of History and Technology.

16 May 1899—Stephen Balzer to Professor Langley

At the suggestion of Mr. J. E. Watkins I take great pleasure in presenting to the National Museum my first automobile carriage. It was built in the year 1894 and ran successfully for six months. I believe it to be the first road carriage driven by a rotating [4] gasoline engine without water jacket.

20 May 1899—Memorandum from George C. Maynard, Curator of the Department of Mechanical Technology, United States National Museum describing Balzer's automobile.

This Balzer machine is a four-wheeled, rubber-tired vehicle, 5 feet 6 inches long; 2 feet 9 inches wide; 3 feet 2 inches high; gas pipe frame; wooden seat and foot-rest. Extra rotary engine with the wagon.

As shown by the accompanying memorandum the wagon was placed in the old Fisheries Hall 12 January 1899 and is still there.[5]

1 September 1899—Waste book [6] entry by Manly

I have today received from Mr. Balzer a small flywheel and a small box of fittings which belong to his "second engine," and have put Pierce to work fitting the engine up. As soon as I can find the time I

---

[4] Refers to a rotary engine.

[5] Another memorandum written by Maynard on 18 November 1905 indicated that an extra Balzer automobile engine was officially given to C. Manly on 5 September 1899. It was used by Manly to familiarize himself with Balzer's design and to conduct aeronautical experiments.

[6] Langley's name for notebooks in which he and his staff kept records of their experiments.

FIGURE 5.—Balzer Automobile of 1894. Now on exhibit at the Smithsonian Institution. (Smithsonian photo A45576-C.)

will have a small carbureter built, so that I can use this engine to drive one of the 2½ meter propellers, and thus get some idea of the power required to obtain a given number of revolutions of them. This engine of Balzer's is said to have developed between 2½ and 3 horse power. I will run it first to make a brake test with a series of R.P.M.'s

11

FIGURE 6.—Engine and transmission of Balzer automobile of 1894 (Smithsonian photo A45576-B.)

and will then attach the propeller to it and note the number of revolutions, and comparing them with the number obtained during the brake test, I will be able to determine the horse power required to drive the propeller at a given speed. After having once obtained data of this kind, I feel very safe in making rough extra-polations up to 15 or 20 horse power, as it is at present we know nothing at all of the power required to drive the propeller at *any speed whatever* and consequently are unable to say whether or not Balzer's engine would drive the propellers at as high a speed as 500 revolutions, even should it develop as much as 20 horse power. I am rather inclined to think that Balzer's engine will not drive both the propellers at 500 revolutions, even should it come up to as much as 20 horse power.

12 September 1899—Another reference to Balzer's spare automobile engine appeared in a letter Manly wrote to Balzer

The fly wheel and fittings for the second engine were received in due time, and I thank you very much for having sent them on, and having placed the engine at my disposal. I am now having the engine fitted up and hope to have it running within a few days. I shall, however, have to have a carbureter built for it, and would like very much to try the plan we were speaking of when I saw you last, that is, to have a small carbureter made out of wired discs and supplied from an ordinary tin vessel. However, as I have had very little occasion to construct carbureters, I would be very glad if you would, just as soon as possible, make a rough sketch showing a tank holding about 1 gallon, with its carbureter, which should be large enough to supply the gas necessary for this "second engine." I do not wish a *scale* drawing, but would like to have you just take a pencil and make a rough sketch, showing a few of the dimensions, so that I can give it in a rough way for the present purpose.

I would also be glad if you would write a letter addressed to Mr. J. E. Watkins, in his official capacity as Curator of Mechanical Technology, U.S. National Museum, directing that the second engine be delivered to me at the Institution. I have already secured the engine, but merely want this letter sent to Mr. Watkins so that the official form may be gone through with.

31 March 1900—A final reference to Balzer's spare automobile engine appeared in a letter Manly wrote to Balzer

In regard to your request that I write up a sort of report of your wagon engine, and send it to Mr. E. Molson, 411 West 147th Street, New York City, I explained to you over the long distance telephone that it would

FIGURE 7.—Cylinder details of Balzer automobile engine of 1894. *Left to right:* Automatic intake valve spring, make and break ignition return spring, and exhaust valve spring. (Smithsonian photo A417.)

be impossible for me to render an *official opinion* upon the engine, as this would be contrary to the wishes of the Secretary *at the present time,* owing to the fact that he wishes the matter kept quiet until after the official test. However, I stated to you over the 'phone that I would be very glad to speak in a personal way, and as a Mechanical Engineer, with regard to your wagon engine, but owing to my official connection with the Institution I prefer not to write to Mr. Molson direct, though

14

FIGURE 8.—Cylinder details of Balzer automobile engine of 1894. *Left to right:* exhaust ports, exhaust tube, intake tube, and ignition wire. (Smithsonian photo A416.) See Figure 7.

if you desire you may show him this letter, calling particular attention to the remarks which I make below concerning it.

I first examined one of your engines during the latter part of November, 1898, and the opinion which I then formed that it was built upon thoroughly correct (both thermodynamic and mechanical) principles has been, I think, entirely justified by what I have seen of your engines since that time.

I consider the principle of the rotating cylinders which you use in their construction as making them particularly well adapted for automobile work, the revolving cylinders making it possible to build an engine for a given horsepower of a very much lighter weight than on any other principle that I know of.

Balzer's automobile engines of 1894 had several features in common with the first stage of the Balzer-Manly Rotary Aero engine of 1900—the first full-size gasoline airplane engine. They are described in Patent Number 573,174 issued to Balzer on 15 December 1896, and are as follows: (1) Rotary radial design, (2) Odd number of cylinders, (3) Air-cooled cylinders, (4) Automatic (suction operated) intake valves, (5) Exhaust valves operated by a cam concentric with the crankshaft, (6) Low tension make-and-break ignition system, (7) Ball and socket joints (pistons to connecting rods), (8) Slipper bearings (connecting rods to crankshaft), (9) Surface carburetion, (10) Four-stroke cycle operating system.

As described in the next chapter, another automobile engine also influenced the design of the Balzer-Manly engine. This was the De Dion-Bouton engine discovered by Langely and Manly while they were in Europe during 1900 seeking an improvement over the Balzer-Manly rotary engine.

Chapter 2

Influence of the De Dion-Bouton
Automobile Engine, 1900

13 May 1899—"The DeDion-Bouton Tricycle," by E. Bernard, Scientific American, *vol. LXXX (19): 307–308.*

Nowhere has the development of automatically propelled vehicles reached a more advanced stage than in France, where, on account of the fine roads and pavements, the most favorable conditions are found for their operation. Carriages and tricycles operated by gasoline motors are now among the ordinary sights in the streets of Paris. Among the latter the tricycle DeDion-Bouton is most extensively in operation, and may be considered as typical of this class of vehicles.

The motive power used is that of a small hydrocarbon motor, operating on the same principle as the gasoline engine, the gas being furnished by the evaporation of gasoline contained in a vaporizing chamber, and then mixed with air to form an explosive mixture, which is then conducted to the chamber of the motor, and which by its explosion at proper intervals operates the piston.

The action of the motor will be seen by referring to the diagram shown in Fig. 1 [Figure 13]. To the left is the vaporizing chamber or carbureter, in which the gasoline contained in the lower half is brought into contact with the air entering by the tube, A, and made to pass between the horizontal plate, B, and the surface of the liquid; the carbureted air then rises, as shown by the arrows, and enters the double valve, C, shown below in detail, by which it is mixed with an additional quantity of air, which enters by the orifice, D, at the top; the mixture then passes to the motor by means of the tube, E. The admixture of air is regulated by the handle on the left, and the supply of gas by that on the right. The float, F, serves to indicate the level of the gasoline in the

FIGURE 9.—De Dion-Bouton engine. View of driveshaft end.
(Smithsonian photo A232–C.)

carbureter by means of a rod which passes through the tube of admission; and the tube itself is arranged to slide up and down in order to maintain a constant difference between the horizontal plate and the surface of the liquid, this plate being attached to the lower end of the tube. In order to avoid the cooling of the gasoline by evaporation, it is warmed by means of the tube, G, through which passes a portion of the hot gas escaping from the motor. By this means a nearly constant temperature is obtained for a given speed of the motor.

The cylinder, H, of the motor is of cast steel, with projecting flanges which serve to increase its radiating surface and prevent overheating; above is the chamber, J, in which the explosion of the gas takes place; at the top of the chamber is the valve, K, which admits the gas coming from the carbureter; the valve is normally closed by means of the spring, S, whose pressure is regulated so as to allow the valve to open upon the descent of the piston. Opposite is the exhaust valve, L, which permits the waste gasses to escape after the explosion; to the valve, L, is attached a rod which passes through the cover of the exhaust chamber and engages with a cam, M, by pushing up the rod, opens up the valve at the proper instant, this valve being normally closed by the spring r. At W is shown the igniter, consisting of two copper rods passing through an insulating bushing and so arranged as to allow a spark from the induction coil to pass in the interior of the chamber for the ignition

18

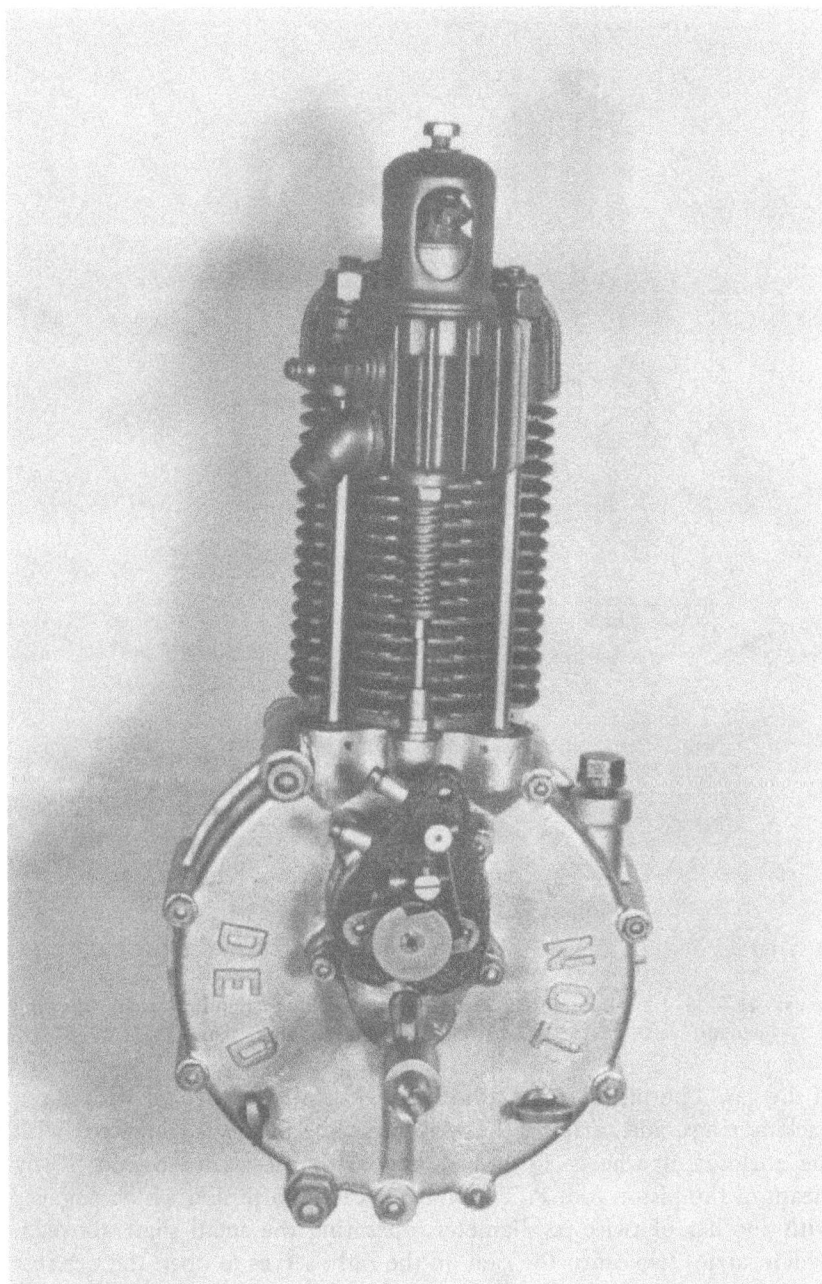

FigURE 10.—De Dion-Bouton engine. View of ignition end. (Smithsonian photo A232.)

19

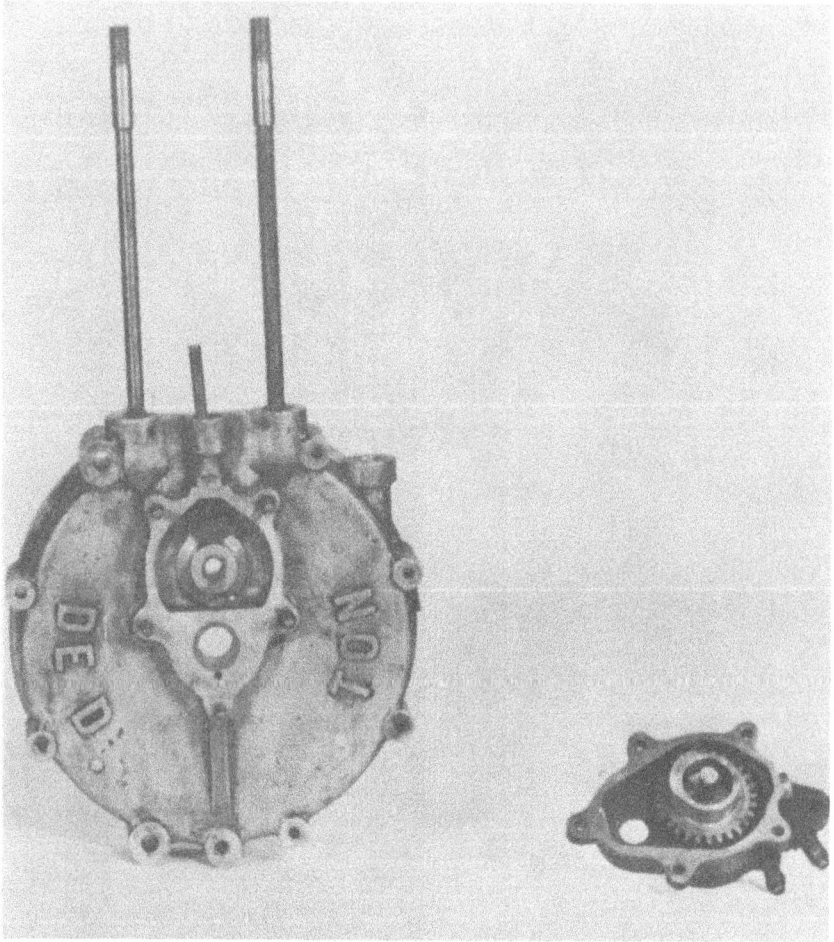

FIGURE 11.—De Dion-Bouton engine. Crankcase section (ignition side) showing exhaust valve cam and cam follower. (Smithsonian photo A4474A.)

of the gas. The piston, O, is a hollow steel casting provided with three packing rings, and carrying the wrist-pin. The piston is connected with the enclosed fly-wheels, Q and R, and with the shafts, S and T, by means of the piston rod, P. The shaft, S, carries a pinion which engages with another of twice its diameter, operating the small shaft above, t, which carries two cams; the cam on the right serves to open the exhaust valve once in every two revolutions, while that to the left acts upon the lever arm, U, carrying the contact, V, of the induction coil, by means of

FIGURE 12.—De Dion-Bouton engine. Left to right: crankcase section (ignition side), cylinder, piston, cylinder head, crankshaft with connecting rod and flywheel unit. (Smithsonian photo A4474.)

which a spark is caused to pass at W, thus igniting the gas contained in the chamber of the motor.

This induction coil is operated by four dry piles. From the preceding description the action of the motor will be readily understood. When the piston descends, it produces a vacuum in the top chamber, by action of which the valve, K, opens, admitting the detonating mixture from the carbureter; when the piston rises, it compresses this gas, and the valve of admission closes. At the instant of the second descent of the piston the cam actuates the lever, making contact with the induction coil, upon which a spark passes, causing an explosion of the gas, which pushes the piston with sufficient force to cause it to pass twice through the same position; when the piston rises after its descent, it compresses the residual gasses of explosion, and at this instant the cam, M, lifts the exhaust valve and the gas leaves the motor by the exhaust pipe, Y. When the piston redescends, this valve closes and the upper valve opens, as before, to admit a fresh supply of gas, and so on.

The action of the motor is thus determined by four different periods, which may be characterized as (1) introduction of gas, (2) compression, (3) explosion, (4) evacuation of the products of combustion.

Figs. 2 and 3 [of Figure 13] show the tricycle complete. In Fig. 2 the handle, D, serves to open or close at the proper time the cock shown in the diagram, Fig. 1, at Z, which permits the piston to ascend and descend freely when starting the motor. The handle, A, displaces the support of the contact of the induction coil in order to vary the instant of ignition with relation to the introduction of gas; the handles, B and C, serve respectively to regulate the admission of gas to the motor and the introduction of air to the carbureter. The pedal, P, operates the main axle of the tricycle and at the same time starts the motor, which is

21

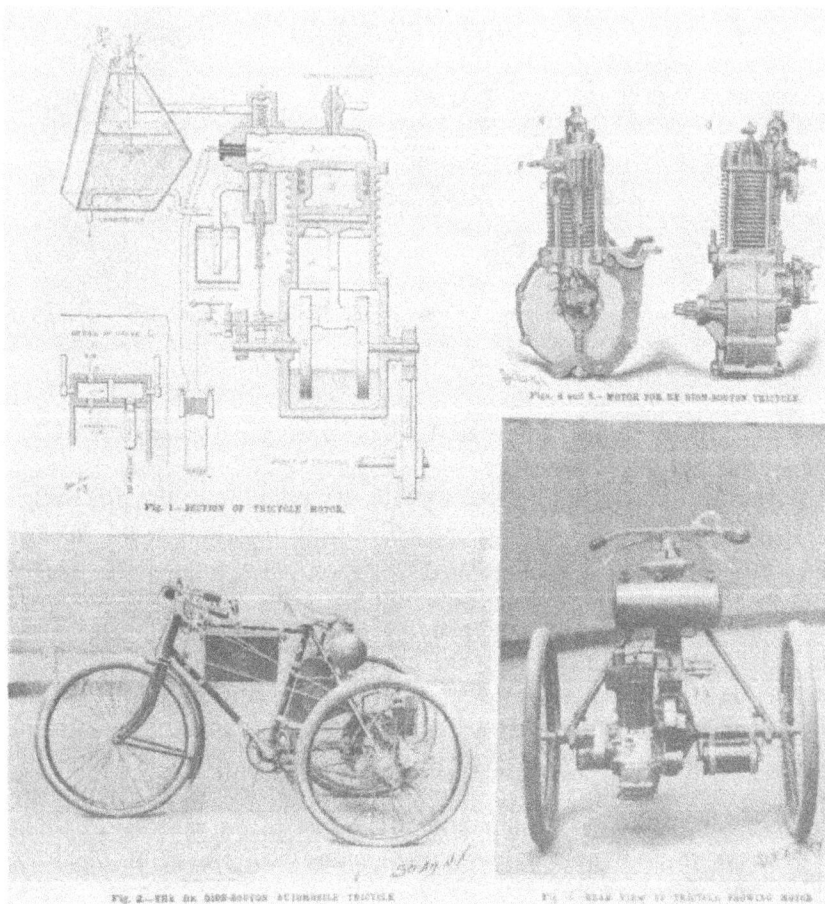

FIGURE 13.—Illustrations from "The De Dion-Bouton Tricycle," by E. Barnard, *Scientific American*, 13 May 1899, LXXX (19) : 307. (Smithsonian photo A20939–A.)

geared to the same axle. The tricycle may be operated by the pedal alone in case of accident or in mounting steep grades.

Figs. 4 and 5 [of Figure 13] show the motor dismounted and provided with a frame for securing it to the tricycle. A is the admission valve; B, igniter; C, exhaust pipe; D, rod and spring of exhaust valve; E, contact, cam and binding posts.

The maximum speed of the tricycle is 24 miles an hour, and grades of eight to ten percent may be mounted without the aid of the pedals.[7]

---

[7] It developed $2\frac{1}{2}$ horsepower.

22

The Waltham Manufacturing Company of Waltham, Massachusetts, will exclusively sell the product of DeDion-Bouton and Company in the United States, and in addition to selling the regular machines now manufactured by DeDion-Bouton and Company they will import the DeDion motors and make a complete line of "Orient" motor cycles and motor carriages. They are now building tricycles, trailers and attachments, tandems, and a light carriage, and will add other vehicles.[8]

2 October 1900—Langley memorandum (in part), Paris, France

I went out to Puteaux to see Mr. Bouton of the De Dion-Bouton firm. Bouton, I was told, is the original engineer and inventor, and De Dion the man of business, although he had learned a good deal of engineering on the way.

Bouton was to be there shortly, but when [we] got out there he had not arrived, and I entered into conversation with a resident engineer whose name was Lecoeur. I got nothing out of him that was practical.

He thought that the firm would try to build something if I wished it, though they would not undertake it in a commercial spirit and not at any fixed price, that is, attempt a machine of 20 horsepower weighing 80 kilos [1 kilogram = approximately 2.2 pounds].

He proposed to show me the parts that were actually in use for the light motors. I went up to the warehouse where the pieces were all arranged.

I understood that in the ordinary way of business, these are only to be bought by those who have machines already, and that the machines themselves cannot be got for a long time, because there are so many orders in advance.

Mr. Lecoeur agreed to deliver to me here tomorrow morning at 9:30 o'clock, completely boxed, the entire engine outfit of a bicycle or tricycle engine. It was to be complete, including the batteries, carbureter and every incident of part. I do not remember the size of the cylinder, but it was I think 3½ inches.

He remarked that the 2½ horsepower could be extended with a somewhat more effective cooling than was obtained by the radiation.

---

[8] It is ironical to note that this copy of *Scientific American* was available to Langley before he left for Europe. In Langley's words the only useful information regarding aeronautical engines garnered by Manly and himself during the European trip was data about the DeDion-Bouton engine plus the fact that one of these engines was imported by the Smithsonian.

Advertisements for the DeDion-Bouton "Motorette" appeared in *Scientific American* for 18 and 25 August and 1 and 8 September 1900. It was called, "The standard automobile motor of the world." Over 20,000 were in actual use.

The whole thing was to be 600 francs, and I undertook to take it as it stood, away with me in the carriage, but he said that it would take some time to box it up and that I might rely with absolute confidence of its being here in the morning.

I was to pay 600 francs in the form of a letter on the banker.

3 October 1900—Langley diary (in part)

The DeDion-Bouton 3 HP engine is delivered at the hotel this morning & S.P.L. pays the carrier 600 francs, getting a receipted bill [$115.80].

1 November 1900—Manly waste book entry (in part)

I today had the small DeDion-Bouton engine taken apart and the various important parts weighed.

The most notable thing about the whole engine is the lightness of the pistons, the wall of the piston being only 2½ millimeters thick, and the head only 4 millimeters thick; the piston rings fit very loosely in their grooves, there being only three rings.

10 November 1900—Wells diary

The account of the DeDion-Bouton Motorette Company for $52.00 was sent them today, also a letter and copy of regulations of the U.S. Treasury requesting them to forward the necessary certificate of authority enabling the proper officer to sign vouchers.

13 November, 1900—Wells diary (in part)

The Secretary was reimbursed to the amount of $115.80 for the small De Dion-Bouton engine which he bought of the manufacturers in Paris in October.

18 January 1901—Wells diary (in part)

The De Dion-Bouton motor is mounted on a testing frame in the lower room of the South Shed, and this morning ran about 4,000 rpm.

Voucher No. 405—Page 21—1901

January 25th–To 5 Spark Plugs [9]–$2.00–$10.00
De Dion-Bouton Motorette Company
37th and Church Lane, Brooklyn, New York
 Signed by Langley and Manly

---

[9] The De Dion-Bouton used one spark plug, however, Langley's aero engines used 5 spark plugs.

20 February 1901–F. W. Hadley in Washington, D.C., to the De Dion-Bouton Motorette Company, 37th and Church Lane, Brooklyn, New York.

I am authorized by the Secretary to inquire whether you can furnish the Institution with some of the porcelain stems as are used in the sparking plugs.

A great deal of difficulty has been experienced at the Institution from these porcelain portions of the plug getting broken, and what is wanted is either the separate porcelain stem or the stem with merely the platinum wire cemented into it.

If you can furnish these please let the Secretary know as soon as possible, and at what price.

Voucher 468–Page 112–1901

    To: De Dion-Bouton Motorette Company
           37th and Church Lane, Brooklyn, New York

Feb. 28th—5 Porcelains for sparking plugs	.20—$1.00
May 8th—15 Porcelains for sparking plugs	.20—$3.00
May 24th—20 Porcelains for sparking plugs	.20—$4.00
	$8.00

[Signed] S. P. Langley

1 May 1901—Wells diary (in part)

The large engine is run considerably today by the attached De Dion-Bouton engine in the process of "wearing" the new pistons.

It is found later today that this D. B. [De Dion-Bouton] engine heats up too rapidly so Mr. Manly has one of the electric motors attached to the engine in its place.

No further mention is made of additional experiments using the De Dion-Bouton engine. Two features of the De Dion-Bouton engine were used in Manly's development of the Balzer-Manly engine; the lightweight pistons and the ignition system.

On 18 February 1901, according to the Wells diary, piston castings were received from the Erie Foundry Company, and were installed on 29 April 1901. Apparently from this time onward only the De Dion-Bouton type of piston was used. Figure 12 illustrates this type of piston which is still in general use today. It is readily distinguished from the design Balzer employed by the fact that it uses a piston pin as opposed to the ball and socket bearing employed by Balzer which is illustrated in Figure 18.

The ignition system is discussed in detail in the affidavits of Hewitt and Newham of 22 and 23 May 1933 (pages 179–183). A quotation follows from the Newham affidavit.

"The make and break ignition system with which said original engine had been equipped by Balzer was not satisfactory, and Mr. Manly instructed us to make a copy of the De Dion jump-spark system that was installed on an engine he had purchased in France from the Comte De Dion. This ignition system was successful."

Balzer had planned to use a high-tension or jump-spark system, but he changed his mind and with Manly's approval installed low-tension ignition.

The Balzer-Manly aero engine underwent modifications for five years through four principal stages of development. These stages may be defined by the horsepower achieved at the end of each modification stage.

The first stage reached a culmination in 1900 when the engine developed 8 horsepower as an aircooled rotary. During the second stage when the engine was changed to a static radial and cooled with damp rags it reached 18 horsepower in 1901. The third stage was reached in 1902 as a result of modern design light weight pistons which permitted the development of 23 horsepower; and 1903 marked the culmination of the fourth stage when 52 horsepower was attained after the engine was equipped with larger cylinders. This progress is charted on Figure 44 (page 185). A detailed description of the stages is given in the following three chapters.

In addition to power-producing modifications, there were two other important improvements which greatly increased the engine's endurance: the addition of permanent water jackets, instead of damp rags, to keep the cylinders cool; and the use of a master and link rod system to replace a less advanced method of joining the pistons with the crankshaft.

Chapter 3

Balzer-Manly Aero Engine, First Stage

During the entire first stage, the engine was in Balzer's machine shop, and its features reflected his thinking. Developed as an aircooled rotary radial, the engine was the simplest, lightest, and most practical form at this state of the art. Although this type became very popular from 1910 through 1920, Balzer was unable to fully develop his own version of the rotary.

22 October 1898—Langley's first entry in his record book

I mean to use this book as a strictly private diary of the more important or to me more interesting parts of what goes on in connection with Aerodromics.

At the time I write, I have had some conferences with the Board of Army and Navy officers appointed by the Secretaries of War and Navy. A copy of their report is in a large envelop in a drawer of my private desk. Nothing has come of it, and nothing may come.

I have decided, however, to go on with the large aerodrome as far as the limited means allow, if I can get a gas engine built within the terms of the proposed contract with the American Motor Company, of New York.

The American Motor Company, after offering to build such a gas engine as I would want, have since then withdrawn from their proposal, and asked a higher price, which was acceded to, and finally after six months delay, have decided they will not undertake. I am about writing to the Pope Manufacturing Company.[10]

The sketch plans for the large aerodrome have been made. The

---

[10] The above paragraph emphasizes the importance of the engine. It was considered to be the major unknown quantity. The American Motor Company gave up when it could not find anyone willing to cast the cylinders.

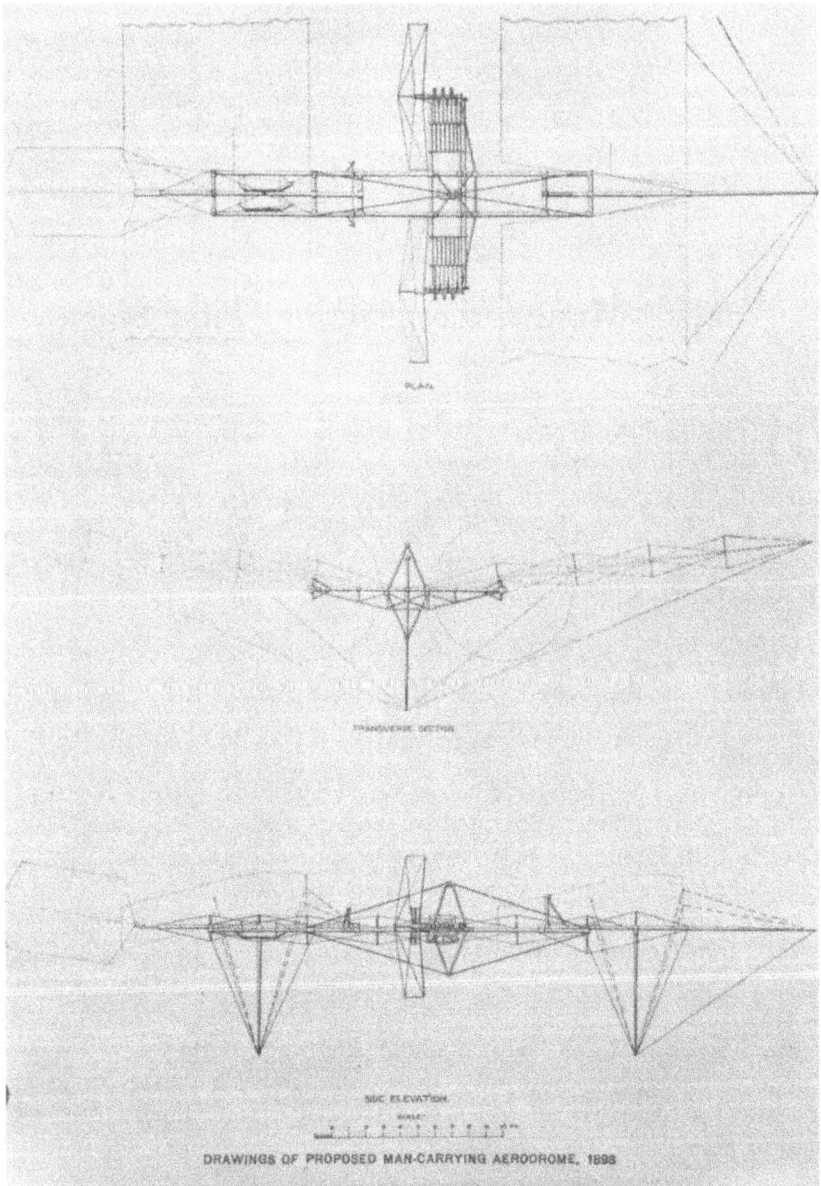

FIGURE 14.—Three views of proposed man-carrying aerodrome drawn by W. L. Speiden on 11 June 1898 under supervision of Langley and Manly. Sent to American Motor Co. From "Langley Memoir on Mechanical Flight" *Smithsonian Contributions to Knowledge,* vol. 27, no. 3 (1911), pl. 32. (Smithsonian photo A33322.)

28

French tubes are all ready, and the brass thimbles for uniting them at least temporarily so that the machine can be set up, are nearly done.[11]

5 November 1898—Letter from Rathbun to Mr. Stephen M. Balzer, at 370 Gerard Avenue, New York City.

The Smithsonian Institution is desirous of promoting the construction of specially light gasoline engines, and the Secretary directs me to inquire whether you would accept an order for one of 12 brake horse power weighing not over 120 pounds, fly wheel, water-jacket and water, or substitutes for water (such as special radiation) and every accessory included. The weight would include a crankshaft but not a bed plate engine mount.

By way of explanation, I might say if it is thought desirable, there may be as many as 6 cylinders as a substitute for the fly wheel or otherwise and that the engine would need to be guaranteed to run three hours without heating. Many usual considerations may be sacrificed to weight.

7 November 1898—Waste book entry by Langley

Lieutenant J. N. Lewis, recorder of the Board of Ordnance and Fortification wrote me on the 2nd of November on the part of the Ordnance Board. He called Saturday, and I showed him the shop and loaned him the photograph of the aluminum ballon with a group of Prussian officers.

He says the Board has had two talks over the report of the Army and Navy officers. He thinks they will be willing to approve the $50,000 if it need not all be given at once. I asked him to prepare them not to expect to see an actual flight of the model (5 or 6) this year. I am to go before the Board on the 9th at 12.[12]

11 November 1898—John F. Stout in New York City to Langley in Washington, D.C.

Replying to your esteemed favor of the 5th inst. would say that we

---

[11] The three-view drawing (Figure 14), previously published in the 1911 *Langley Memoir on Mechanical Flight*, shows the aerodrome powered with two six-cylinder inline engines mounted on outriggers, each one directly driving a propeller. This arrangement had the advantage of simplicity; however, it was a heavier installation than having the engines mounted inboard and driving the propellers by means of chains or shafts. It was presently decided that the additional weight of the bracing needed to support the engines when mounted on outriggers was too great a penalty to pay. As a result all of the later designs show inboard mounted engine (s) .

[12] Langley did go before the Board as scheduled, and received an immediate appropriation of $25,000.

would undertake to build a gasoline engine that would develop 12 brake horse power and not weigh more than 120 pounds, and would take an order for one, providing that we can get a satisfactory price. You will of course understand that as it would have to be made specially it would be quite expensive, but we would guarantee it in every particular and give a fine mechanism. There is no question but that it will not heat if run 24 hours and at a high speed.

We would be pleased to hear from you further on this subject and would esteem it a great honor to secure your order.

12 November 1898—Rathbun in Washington, D.C., to Stout in New York City.

Your letter of the 11th instant, in regard to the proposed small gasoline engine, has been received, and, in reply, the Secretary directs me to say that the engine desired must fulfill the following specifications:

The engine is to be an Otto cycle, six cylinder gasoline engine, capable of developing 12 brake horse power at from 600 to 800 revolutions per minute, but working efficiently at any speed between 400 and 1,200 revolutions per minute, of a total weight not to exceed 120 pounds, including crank-shaft, flywheel, water-jacket and water, or substitutes for water (such as special radiation) and every other accessory except bed-plate.

The 12 brake horse power in question shall be developed continuously, with ordinary careful handling, by an ordinary engineer, and the engine must be capable of being run continuously for three hours without overheating. The engine must be capable of burning ordinary gasoline, and the fuel consumption is not to exceed one pound per horse power per hour.

I am further directed to say that only responsible parties have been written to with reference to this proposed engine, and, if it be decided to build it, that the contract will be let to the lowest bidder, with the understanding that it will not be received until a rigorous and satisfactory inspection has been made of everything used in the construction of and the workmanship on the engine, as well as of its fulfillment of the preceeding condition under tests.

The engine must be completed and ready for the official test within four months from the date of the contract, and this test shall be held in Washington, in the presence of three experts, one to be appointed by each party and the third by mutual agreement.

If you care to enter into a contract containing the above specifications, an illustrative drawing will be sent you showing the method of support and general disposition of the cylinders. However, in order to enable this illustrative sketch to be prepared, you should send a sketch showing the approximate dimensions of the cylinder and the length of the stroke which you would use. If you care to, further make an estimate on a still lighter engine, specifying weight and price.

9 May 1898—Langley in Washington, D.C., to R. H. Thurston in Ithaca, New York.

I mention in especial confidence that official enquiries from the Army and Navy lead me to think it possible (I can hardly say probable) that an aerodrome capable of a speed of 30 miles an hour maintained for three hours, carrying an "aeronaut" and possibly some missiles may be attempted. I think it practicable though not to be realized without trial. I should try to have some form of gas engine. Have you any young man who is morally trustworthy ("a good fellow") with some gumption and a professional training.[13] If nothing comes of this, I have still some work for such a one in experimenting here, on aerodynamic data, etc.

26 November 1898—book Entry by Langley

The Balzer engine (mounted on a tricycle) arrived yesterday afternoon and Manly is testing its hp today.[14]

1 December 1898—Manly and Watkins to Langley

In connection with the accompanying memoranda, I beg to recommend that unless some better offer should be received for the gas engine from other manufacturers, the contract be closed with Mr. Balzer, if he will accept it on the terms already proposed, and if his price is reasonable.

30 November 1898—Memorandum from Manly to Langley (in part)

Mr. Balzer had come down to bid on a gas engine of 12 horse power weighing not over 120 pounds and fulfilling the other conditions incorporated in the letter to him of November fifth. Mr. Balzer now finds that the weight is limited to 100 pounds for 12 horse power, and he is

---

[13] Dr. Thurston chose Charles Matthews Manly who did not even wait to be graduated properly—his diploma was granted in absentia. On 1 June 1898, he reported (sight unseen) to Langley in Washington, D.C., signed the pay roll for $1,000 per annum, and presently became "aide in aerodromics."

[14] Langley, Manly, and Balzer became directly involved on the aero engine project for the first time. From this consortium evolved the most advanced airplane engine in the world at the turn of the century.

therefore, at the present moment unprepared to put in his bid without further calculations of weights, cost, etc. Mr. Balzer's intention was to construct the engine upon the principles of the other engines which he sent down here, the only difference being that he now proposes to use 5 cylinders instead of 3. By using 5 cylinders he is able to obtain 5 explosions for 2 revolutions of the engine, thus leaving no portion of the stroke dead. This latter construction would be quite a gain, since the engine will run very much smoother.

In the construction of his 5 cylinder engine Mr. Balzer proposes to make the cylinders $4\frac{1}{4}$ inches in diameter, with a 6 inch stroke. The cylinder proper are to be made of $\frac{1}{16}$ inch soft steel, with a cast iron

FIGURE 15.—Jacobs engine of 1914 illustrating the use of both spiral and parallel types of cooling fins. (Smithsonian photo A607.)

bushing 1/8 inch thick. On the outside of these steel cylinders he will turn screw threads, to facilitate cooling by radiation. The object in turning a screw thread on these cylinders, instead of parallel rings, is that the screw thread will tend to conduct the heat from the hot end of the cylinder to the cooler end, whereas the rings would not do so.[15] In building his engine for 120 pounds weight Mr. Balzer had expected that the cylinders would weigh 8½ pounds each, and that the pistons would weigh about 1 pound each. The length of the bearing surface of the piston would have a square section. Mr. Balzer expects to cut down the weight of these cylinders now, in order to bring the weight of the engine within 100 pounds. This he will do by making the steel less than $1/16$ of an inch in thickness. He does not care to cut down the thickness of the cast iron bushing, because the cast iron, being a porous metal, absorbs oil, and thus lubricates the piston, and he fears that less than 1/8 of an inch will not be a sufficient thickness for this purpose.

This 5 cylinder engine will have no [fly] wheel surrounding it at all, being in this respect similar to the first engine which Mr. Balzer sent on here.

Mr. Balzer says that the premature explosion occurs when the cylinders reach a temperature of about 650 Fah[renheit]. He also says that he is not worried at all in regard to keeping the cylinders cool without the use of a water jacket; his idea in arranging these cylinders in a circle, and allowing them to revolve, is to obviate this very difficulty.

Mr. Balzer expects to obtain a pressure of 350 pounds to the square inch at the beginning of the explosion. This will necessitate very accurate fitting of the pistons to the cylinders. He proposes to use 5 cast iron packing rings on the piston, the centre ring being a bull-ring.

The cylinders of the engine will describe a circle about 33 inches in diameter. The central drum on which the 5 cylinders are to be mounted will be about 12 inches in diameter, and will be constructed of steel, and every precaution will be taken to make it as light and at the same time as strong as possible.

Mr. Balzer does not propose to use a coil for sparking the cylinders, but will construct a small high voltage dynamo which will be placed on the same shaft with, and very close to, the engine. The dynamo itself will weigh about 5½ pounds, and it will cost him about $100.00 to have it built. He will have the dynamo built outside by an electrical concern, but after his own designs.

---

[15] The reference is to different types of cooling fins, one featuring a spiraling type such as used on some air-cooled machine guns, and the other a series of parallel rings as used on all modern air-cooled aero engine cylinders.

He does not now use a "wiping contact" for igniting the charge in the cylinders, but uses instead an arrangement by which he gets a spark at the proper time.[16]

Mr. Balzer was unable to give me an exact estimate as to the time required to build the engine under the modified conditions, but he said that it would require between 3 and 4 months.

Owing to the fact that the cylinders of the engine will sweep through a circle of something more than 30 inches diameter, I beg to advise, for several reasons (which we have already discussed), that the engine be so placed in the aerodrome that the plane of the circle described by the cylinders will be in the direction of motion of the aerodrome. If the engine is thus placed it will present a surface of only about 1 square foot, perpendicular to the direction of motion of the aerodrome, since the engine will be only about 5 inches wide. If the engine is placed directly on the propeller shaft it will present a surface of nearly 6 square feet, perpendicular to the direction of motion of the aerodrome. Mr. Balzer does not feel certain that he can guarantee the 12 brake horse power without providing for possibly more, as no skill or knowledge will enable one to calculate the horse power of a gas engine accurately in advance. The horse power depends so much on the degree to which compression of the explosive mixture is carried, and compression depends so much on the tightness of the pistons in the cylinders, that it is very difficult to say just what horse power will be developed with a given size of gas engine running at a given speed.

I add a rough sketch to illustrate the principle of construction which Mr. Balzer employs in his gas engines.[17]

If the crank is fixed, the cylinders kick themselves and the supporting-drum backwards, and if the cylinders are fixed the crank is kicked forward, so that no matter which is fixed, power may be obtained from the other.

I consider the principle of construction which he employs in his engine as both mechanically and thermodynamically correct, and I beg to say that my opinion is that the engine which you desire can be constructed very much lighter on this principle than on any other which I have seen.

I find Mr. Balzer a practical mechanic who can build (and perhaps will build) this engine with his own hands, and who appears to under-

---

[16] By "wiping contact" Manly means a low tension ignition system. The implication is that Balzer proposed a high tension or spark plug ignition system which is the modern practice.

[17] Not reproduced here.

stand and appreciate the thermodynamical and mechanical principles involved in the construction of gas engines. According to his statement (confirmed by Mr. J. E. Watkins) he has a large and well equipped shop which is devoted to the manufacture of a number of engineering appurtenances, but which is capable of being used in the construction of gas engines. Mr. Balzer is evidently desirous to build this engine and appears very much interested in the work. You have seen Mr. Balzer and will perhaps agree with me the favorable impression that he has made on Mr. Watkins and myself.

5 December 1898—Balzer in New York City to Langley in Washington, D.C.

My interview with Mr. Watkins and Mr. Manly about the proposed engine. Would say I would be willing to build a fine revolving cylinder gas engine of my own design, developing at five hundred revolutions twelve brake horse power weighing not over one hundred pounds for the sum of $1,500. The workmanship can be passed upon by any mechanic you may appoint. To be delivered ten weeks from date of contract. Hoping this will meet with your approval.

10 December 1898—Rathbun in Washington, D.C., to Balzer in New York City

In reply to your letter of December 5, containing your bid on the proposed 100 pound, 12 horse power, gasoline engine, I am directed by the Secretary to say that your bid will be accepted upon the signing of the enclosed contract and your furnishing the bond for the advance payment therein mentioned.

As soon as you sign the contract please return it and it will be properly signed here and a certified copy will be immediately sent to you.

As the Secretary is about leaving Washington for some weeks, and wishes to dispose of the matter before going away, allow me to request that you attend to the matter as soon as is possible.

12 December 1898—Balzer in New York City to Langley in Washington, D.C.

Find enclosed contract signed. I will forward bond in a few days. Have also put work on engine in hand. Hoping this will meet with your approval, and thanking you for your valued contract.[18]

---

[18] Realizing that Balzer had signed the contract, Langley wrote the Board of Ordnance and Fortification on the same day accepting the invitation to build a man-carrying aerodrome.

17 December 1898—Langley entry in waste book

Yesterday received the following telegram from Lieutenant Lewis, recorder of the Board of Ordnance and Fortification: "Board approved letter. You are given fullest discretion in the work."

Immediately proceeded to arrange, as far as possible, for the work of the New Year.

23 December 1898—Rathbun to George Wells

The Secretary directs me to notify you that as part of your new duties you will have immediate care, under the direction of Mr. Manly, of the books, manuscripts and other papers in the Aerodromic Room, and will also attend to pasting in the scrap books the clippings relating to aerodromics.

The Secretary also wishes me to remind you that your new duties will ordinarily call for a longer day's work than the old ones, as your hours will necessarily be nearly the same as those of the workshops, where you will have frequently to be rather than those of the Parent Institution.

11 January 1899—Langley in Washington, D.C., to Balzer in New York City

I herewith enclose you, in compliance with your verbal request, a sketch showing the general disposition of the engine. You will observe that the sketch provides for the possibility of two engines, but the second engine, if ordered, will come later, and you will notice (1) that the one with which we are concerned at present, must run both propellers if desired; (2) possibility of this second engine must be arranged for so that the propellers can be run by the second, if wished.

As I understand the construction of your engine, it does not, without modifications, admit of the cylinders rotating and yet driving a shaft which is run through continuously in the way here shown, or in some way which will be equally simple and especially equally light.

These are the principle points which I have thought it best to refer to you, who are the designer of the engine and know best how to adapt it to such a condition as here presents itself. I may add incidentally that a desirable provision, but not an absolutely indispensable one, would be to enable the engineer to employ one engine on one propeller wheel, and not on both, if occasion arose. I suppose, however, that this might add weight enough to be prohibitory.[19]

---

[19] Langley was apparently trying to increase maneuverability by being able to speed up one propeller relative to the other.

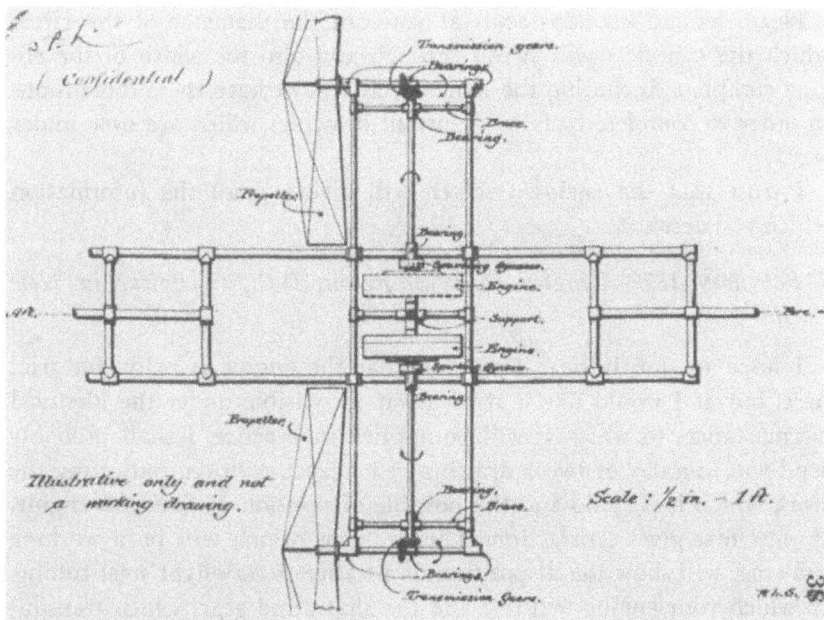

FIGURE 16.—Sketch authorized by Manly, drawn by Speiden, approved by Langley, and forwarded to Balzer on 11 January 1899 showing proposed mounting of engine. (Smithsonian photo A4480-C.)

It will also be noted that the bearings for supporting the engine shaft are not shown, as these are details which will have to be arranged for later, when the exact dimensions of the engine, shaft, etc., are known.

The sketch, which is merely to illustrate in a general way the length of the shaft that will be required to transmit the power from the engine to both propellers, is fully labeled, and arrows indicating the direction of motion of the propellers have been added. The distance between the tubing which forms the cross frame has been made 36 inches, based upon your statement made when you were in Washington, that the diameter of the circle swept through by the engine cylinders would be about 33 inches. If this distance of 36 inches is not great enough to accomodate your engine you should let me know immediately, so that in making up the drawings this can be altered.

The distance between the tubes of the main frame is seen to be 36 inches and it is hoped that this width will accommodate two engines of your design, including their sparking dynamos, but if not let me know by return mail.

37

Please let me know as soon as you can the diameter of the circle which the cylinders will sweep through and also the width of the engine complete, including the dynamo, as I must have these dimensions in order to complete certain important drawings which are now under way.

I trust that the enclosed sketch will give you all the information which you desire.[20]

7 February 1899—Langley in Washington, D.C., to Balzer in New York City

I hope to shortly hear from you that the engine is ready for trial here, but as I would like it tried as far as possible under the identical circumstances to which it will be applied in practice, I shall probably send you in a day or two a drawing of its exact position, indicating the work which it is to do and the possible disposition of a second engine, if your first gives satisfaction. The drawing, which will be a working drawing, will show the disposition of a frame of very light steel tubing, in which your engine will rest and the shafts and gears which transmit its motion to a propeller wheel.

I may ask you to fit up at my expense the driving shafts, gears and accessories (which form no part of your stipulated weight) and also the frame of steel tubing which holds them, and I shall in this case, send you the necessary gears cut, and finishing yourself the minor accessories, so that your engine can be tested under the conditions of actual work, and I can better judge the possible desirability of ordering a second engine. The engines will, of course, be paid for, when the stipulated test is met, but there is something more than this, and perhaps I may add (what I believe you already understand), that these engines are for a very special and confidential purpose.

If they turn out a success, (and success can only be proven by a trial under the conditions of actual motion through the air) I shall think it fair to you, to give as full publicity as I can to the fact that you were the builder, but until the trial under the conditions of actual flight has been made, I shall not feel that success has been proven. Everything that lies in my power will be done to hasten the time when this can be

---

[20] On 16 January 1899 Balzer sent Langley a full size drawing of the engine. Unfortunately it has been lost; however, a good deal is known about the engine as it left Balzer's shop more than a year later due to photographs, patent office drawings, written descriptions by Manly, and studies of Balzer's model aero engine and his automobile engine of 1894.

determined, but until then, I will ask you to join me in keeping the details of this matter as a confidential trust.

9 February 1899—Balzer in New York City to Langley in Washington, D.C.

Your favor of the 7th inst. received, and in reply I would say I expect to give the engine a trial next week. So far all work is satisfactory and hope the engine will fit all requirements. As to the other work you mention, I would be pleased to receive any work that you may entrust to me, and will give it my fullest attention to make it satisfactory. And I can assure you all work done by me will be kept strictly confidential as you requested.

26 February 1899—Langley waste book entry

Mr. Manly reports Balzer's engine likely to develop 20 or more horse. The entire central part of the frame from Pope tube steel with gears is to be built by Balzer, and is likely to be ready for testing here under actual conditions of support by March 20. The delay arises from the construction of this frame.

29 March 1899—Langley at the Metropolitan Club, New York City, to Rathbun in Washington, D.C.

Say to Manly I have seen Balzer's engine and am much pleased by it. Balzer wants the frame strengthened by some bracing and modification of the piece carrying the propeller shaft, and is addressing me a letter here, which I will perhaps forward tomorrow.

If time press, this modification may be made, if Manly approve, especially as Balzer believes his engine can be worked for ten or fifteen minutes up to 30 horse.

He will have it on (he says) next week.

9 May 1899—Manly memorandum to Langley

Mr. Balzer called me up over the 'phone yesterday afternoon at about 5:30 o'clock. He said that he was going to run his shops until 10 o'clock last night and finish up the frame work, and that he would ship it (that is, the frame work) early this morning. The engine is not quite complete, as he finds he will have to put the radiating fins on the cylinders and explosion chambers in order to keep them cool during the 3 hour test. He says that he thinks it will take about a week to complete the engine. He himself is coming down on the train which reaches here at 8 p.m. today. I will see him tonight, and will bring him down to the Institution in the morning.

39

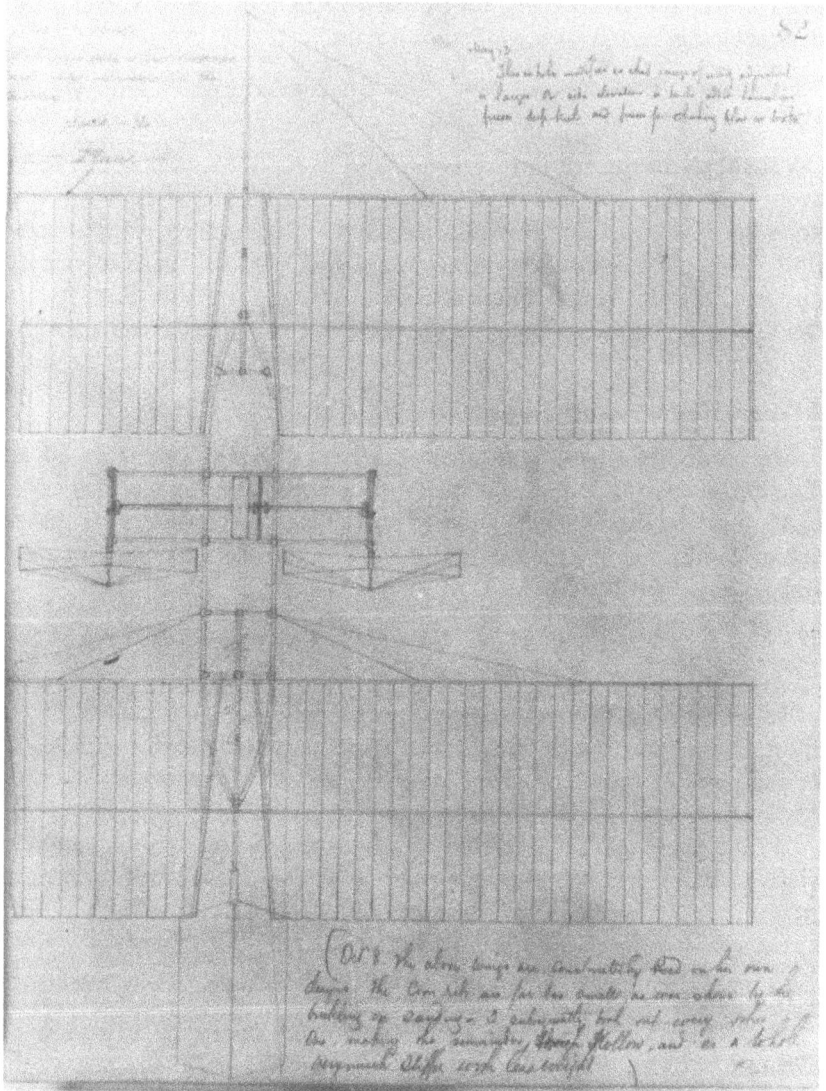

FIGURE 17.—"Preliminary sketch of Great aerodrome made under instructions from the Secretary."Drawn by Speiden, 5 May 1899. (Smithsonian photo A50245.)

23 June 1899—Manly in Washington, D.C., to Langley in Europe (in part)

Nothing further has been heard from Balzer since my last communication to you, but I hope to stir Balzer up now in a short time by inquiries made in a personal way. He seems to have no idea of the value of time, and I hope to impress on him the fact that if he hopes to get any glory out of his engine, that time is growing *more* precious every day. This engine of his *must* be made to do the work, if it necessitates bringing it here to finish it. *If* he cannot build it, I know of *no* company in this country that *would* be able to do it. It is a larger and harder affair than Balzer had any suspicion of. However, I have hopes that he will *yet* fulfill his contract on it.

9 July 1899—Manly in Washington, D.C., to Langley in Europe (in part)

I beg leave to submit the following report on the condition of the work in aerodromics on July 8th 1899:

On July 8th I received a personal letter from Mr. Balzer with reference to the progress he is making with the engine and give you below a copy of it.

"Your favor of July third received and am more than pleased that you have again broken the long silence.

No doubt you know under what difficulties I am laboring. I have been obliged to place the backing-off device for sale in order to raise the neccessary capital to continue work on the engine, and I hope to be successful in doing so.

As far as the engine is concerned, for you, I find that it is necessary to have two three inch cylinders instead of one four and three sixteenths in order to get greater radiating area, and avoid all angles in ports; all ports in cylinders must have an easy entrance without angles to avoid the accumulation of heat; it is not necessary to change any other part of the engine but the cylinders, placing two three inch cylinders side by side with one connecting rod and only one exploding chamber for the two cylinders, the pistons of the two cylinders will be connected together; it is also necessary to have very large ports and valves to get the high speed required. As far as the power of the engine is concerned it will go even beyond my expectations and I will endeavor to do my best and strain every point to deliver the engine to you this month."

As the above is somewhat obscure, I will endeavor to explain it to you. What Balzer means by using two 3 inch cylinders instead of one $4\frac{3}{16}$ inch diameter, is that whereas he originally built the engine with five cylinders, of 4 $3/16$ inches in diameter, arranged equidistantly on the circumference of the supporting drum, he now finds that he will have to substitute ten cylinders, of three inches in diameter, with them arranged in pairs, and placed at five equidistant points on the same drum.

With this arrangement he will have ten pistons and piston rods and five connecting rods, two piston rods being connected together and working on one connecting rod.

If the above is a correct interpretation of what Balzer intends doing, I must say that I somewhat question the advisability of such a mechanical construction. However, I prefer not to render final opinion on the matter without seeing Balzer and finding out *exactly* what he intends to do. Again, I have been quite concerned for some weeks as to whether Balzer was acting fairly about the matter and I have been trying to arrange matters here, so that I could run up to New York and see just what he is doing. However, the work at Quantico has been progressing so very slowly and so little has been accomplished in the time allotted for its completion, that I have felt that no time could be spared for attending to Balzer, until the experiments with the aerodromes were brought to a close, but as it now appears that this may be some time longer, I have decided to go to New York tonight and see Balzer tomorrow, returning to Washington Monday night or early Tuesday morning in order that no time may be lost from the Quantico work.

The "Backing-off device" which Balzer says he has placed on the market is a patented mandrel of his for relieving the teeth of milling cutters. What he says about "having had to place it on the market to raise capital to complete the engine", is all "stuff" and means nothing.

14 July 1899—Manly in Washington, D.C., to Langley in Europe (in part)

I beg leave to make the following report of the condition of the work in aerodromics on July 14, 1899:

In my report of July 9th, I informed you of my intention to go to New York to investigate the condition of the engine which is being built by Mr. Balzer. I left Washington on the night of July 9th, arriving in New York on the following morning and went immediately to Balzer's shops. I had intentionally not informed Balzer of my coming, and so of course my visit was entirely unexpected. I found him at work with two assistants on his 4 hp engine which he uses in his automobile. He was at that time carrying on some investigations with different forms of sparking devices, and informed me that he had been doing so for some weeks.

The engine which he has been building for you was in exactly the same condition as on my previous visit of April 29th.

Mr. Balzer told me that the cause of delay is that before putting the sparking devices for your engine in the explosion chambers he felt it necessary to make some further experiments using one of his heavier engines, and that this was what he had been doing for the last few weeks and which he had now about completed. He said that he did not wish to bore into the very light explosion chambers of your engine until he had satisfied himself as to what was the best form of sparking device, as the engine would require almost a total rebuilding if he should happen to find afterwards that the sparking device should have been put in different positions in the explosion chambers, and also that he was not completely satisfied as to just what is the best form of sparking device to use.

Mr. Balzer's original intention was to use a "jumping" spark for igniting the gas in the explosion chambers, and when he first undertook the building of the engine, I advised him against this as my experience has been that the "jumping" spark is not so reliable as the "wiping" spark, but as Mr. Balzer had had a great deal more experience with gasoline engines, and especially with this form of his own, I of course at that time yielded this point to him. However, Mr. Balzer has now found that the "jumping" spark will not be at all satisfactory for this engine, and he has determined to put in a "wiping" spark as I had originally advised him to do. It is on this very point that he has been making his experiments, and also lately he has been continuing his experiments to try to secure a "wiping" spark which would be absolutely reliable at the very high number of revolutions at which the engine would be required to run to produce the required power.[21]

I found out, however, that the carrying out of these experiments, which are necessary, but at the same time which could not possibly have consumed all of Mr. Balzer's time since my last visit there, was not the principal cause of the delay in the completion of your engine. This delay is principally due to the fact that Mr. Balzer is at a complete financial standstill. He has no mechanics at all at work in his large shops, except the two which he had assisting him in the above experiments. He has a large number of orders, which he showed me, for his automobiles, but he has no money to stand the expenses of the shop and buy the necessary materials for their construction. He informed me that he had spent all of his capital, outside of a private income all of which he required for his living expenses, on the development of his engine and the automobile. He stated, however, that he expects to

---

[21] The "jumping" or "high tension" ignition system offered a greater development potential; however, the "wiping" or "low tension" system offered greater reliability at that time. In its final form the engine was equipped with a "high tension" system. See also footnote 16.

have some money coming in very soon and that he would then push your engine to completion as rapidly as possible. I then told him that he had been promising the completion of the engine for several months, and that you had left this country under the impression that the engine would certainly be delivered before the latter part of May, and that you would be returning now very soon, and would be expecting to find the whole thing completed, and I therefore wanted to urge upon him the necessity of letting me have the engine as soon as possible, as I must get things in shape before your return. After talking to him awhile on this line, he promised me *most emphatically* that he would certainly push the engine through and have it delivered before the first of August, even though it proved necessary to change the construction of the engine by using the ten small cylinders instead of the five larger ones, the plan of which I informed you in my last communication. I fear, however, very greatly, after having been disappointed by him as to the date of delivery so often, that he will not have it finished by that time.

Mr. Balzer wanted to know if it would be possible to have some more money advanced to him, to be secured by a bond, but I informed him that it was contrary to the rules of the Government to pay any money for materials or work until the actual delivery of the same; and that the money which you had advanced to him at the beginning of the work had been advanced from a private fund, and to do this again would be impossible now.

To sum the whole matter up, Balzer is evidently very anxious to complete the engine, but has not the money to carry on the work, and unless he can get it from outside, or can secure some job work of some kind, the running of his shops will be impossible for some time. He is trying to secure partnership with someone having the necessary capital for the placing of his automobile on the market, and although he has had several offers from "promoters" to form the necessary company, yet he is not willing to go into that kind of a company, as he fears that he will not only lose his time, but also his very valuable patents which he holds on his engine and his automobile. He is evidently "waiting for something to turn up". That the man is a master mechanic there is no doubt, and that he has a very wonderful engine there is also no doubt, but he seems utterly lacking in business ability, and is afraid to enter into the formation of any very large company, but desires to deal with some one man who has the necessary capital for the development of the work. As this man seems to be lacking, his very excellently equipped shops are consequently at a standstill. I hope that he may be able to secure the necessary money to complete the engine by the first of next month, but I must confess that I have very little grounds for expecting that it will be accomplished.

21 July 1899—Manly in Washington, D.C., to Langley in Europe (in part)

In my communication of July 14th, in referring to the condition in which I found the engine which Mr. Balzer is building, I neglected to state that while I was in New York City with Mr. Balzer, I urged him to at least put together one cylinder of the engine, attaching it to the crankshaft, and to make an experiment with it so as to be able to determine immediately and definitely whether the present cylinders which he has will be suitable for the engine, or whether it will require the rebuilding of the cylinders. Mr. Balzer promised that he would do this and would let me know the results of the test by Wednesday, July 12th. Thursday, July 13, I received the following note from Balzer:

"It was my intention to send you a few lines last evening, but was unable to finish the one cylinder and advise you of the result. It was too late today when we got through with it and we had very little time to give it a thorough test. I think the cylinders I have are going to answer the purpose, only the ports are a trifle small to give good results.

Tomorrow I put on the drag power and after adjusting all parts will again give it another test and will report results to you.[22]

I have had my wagon out twice, and it runs most satisfactorily."

I have heard nothing further than the above from Mr. Balzer so am unable to state what results were obtained with the one cylinder. I have written to him again to let me know immediately if possible, what results he obtained.

I am rather at a loss to explain how it is that one day Mr. Balzer thinks the present cylinders will work, and the next day he thinks that the engine will have to be rebuilt,—neither of these opinions being supported by any test whatever. If the ports *are* too small to allow the exploded gases to enter and leave the cylinder with a great enough rapidity at the very high speed, then all the cylinders *will* have to be rebuilt, but whether the ports are too small or not can only be determined by test, and this test is the thing I am trying to get Mr. Balzer to make *immediately*. He had abandoned work on the engine, claiming that he found that the ports were too small and that the cylinders would have to be rebuilt, but he had made no experiment whatever, and in fact had

---

[22] This means he was going to put the engine on a prony brake to test its brake horsepower.

45

not even attached the valve gear to any of the cylinders to see what they would do.

As I have stated before, I am convinced, in order to have the engine completed immediately, some arrangement will have to be made by which Mr. Balzer can be advanced some more money to carry on the work. Of course this seems like bad business policy, but at the same time, under the circumstances, I think it will be absolutely necessary.

28 July 1899—Manly in Washington, D.C., to Langley in Europe (in part)

As I informed you in my communication of July 21st, I wrote another personal letter to Mr. Balzer urging him to make the test on the one cylinder of the engine as soon as possible so that I might know immediately something definite in regard to it.

On July 26th, I received the following telegram: "Can make cylinders do. Will write."

I have not yet received this letter so am at present unable to say anything further in regard to the matter. I will communicate to you the contents of Mr. Balzer's letter immediately upon receipt of it.

In regard to the possible necessity of falling back on the steam engine, I must say that I have no fears of such a contingency. A suitable gasoline engine not only *can* but *must* and *will* be built. It may prove necessary to add to the combustion chambers of the engine some small water jackets, and have a small condenser which will handle a *very* few pounds of water, but this would be as nothing compared to the necessity of constructing a steam engine with its complicated generating and condensing auxiliaries. A gasoline engine which will mark the greatest advance in explosion motor construction will be built for the machine.

Allow me to assure you that your expression of confidence in the conduct of the work entrusted is most highly appreciated.

4 August 1899—Manly in Washington, D.C., to Langley in Europe

I have today received the following letter from Mr. Balzer with reference to the engine:

"Yours of the first instant is at hand, I am now hard at work completing the engine being perfectly satisfied with the result of running the cylinder, it seems as close as I can come to it that the compression is 60 and the explosion 180. The explosion chamber does not overheat, but the head of the cylinder gets so hot that I have premature explosion in about 15 minutes but I am quite certain that after the radiating fins

46

are attached the circulation of air will reduce the temperature of the cylinders for their continuous working: the engine in all its construction is perfectly strong enough and I doubt very much whether you will need another engine as this one cylinder develops 4 hp."

What Mr. Balzer means by saying that "the compression is 60 and explosion 180" is that he gets a compression of 60 pounds to the square inch, and that the pressure at the instant of explosion is 180 pounds to the square inch. He does not say at what speed the one cylinder was working when he obtained the 4 brake horsepower from it, so that I am unable to apply any check on the calculations to see whether he has over-estimated the result or not. If one cylinder working by itself has developed 4 horsepower, then with 5 cylinders working, (owing to the fact that with 5 cylinders you have no dead points to the stroke) he should obtain slightly more than 20 horsepower. If Mr. Balzer had not given me reason to rather fear that he over-estimates good results, I would feel perfectly safe in saying that this one engine when completed will be able to furnish all the power which will be required. What I am trying to do now is to make him *complete* the engine so that you can immediately know exactly what is to be expected of it, and I consider the completion of the engine as the *most* urgent part of the work now on hand. If the engine will run in a close space for fifteen minutes before premature explosion occurs, it will certainly run indefinitely if it is allowed to travel with its machine through the air, and I shall therefore spare no effort to force the completion of it immediately.[23]

21 August 1899—Waste Book entry by Manly (in part)

On Monday morning August 21, I went out to Mr. Balzer's shop at 370 Gerard Avenue, New York City having intentionally not informed him of my coming. I found Mr. Balzer at work assisted by two mechanics turning up the valves for the combustion chambers of the engine. The engine was mounted on two heavy cast iron bearing plates which were in turn bolted to the large square drill press which was bolted to the floor. The gasoline tank and carbureter had been disconnected, and being the ones belonging to his automobile, had been replaced in it. The electric connection for the sparking device had also been disconnected. The engine, however, was as it had been when he made his test of the one cylinder of it, the cylinder which had been fitted up with its

---

[23] Both Balzer and Manly should have added that since the engine was designed to be run as a rotary, vastly improved cooling would be realized upon completion of the entire engine. Manly's prediction that the engine had a potential of more than 20 h.p. was actually realized at his hands as will be seen in Chapter 4.

valve being held fast, and pointing directly downward by clamping up the bearings. On that part of the shaft which is connected with the flange of the supporting drum, was placed a large flywheel about 3 feet in diameter, and weighing perhaps 250 lbs. Out beyond this was a small wheel of perhaps 12 in. diameter with a 1 in. face, which he had used for applying his Prony brake.[24]

Mr. Balzer first turned the engine over once or twice by hand, and the steam gauge which he had attached to the combustion chamber showed a compression of 65 lbs. when turned by hand, the needle of the gauge going the same place every time he turned the cylinder so as to get compression.

I had him turn the cylinders of the engine so that I could see the head of the cylinder which had been run, and found that it was somewhat "purpled" by the excessive heating which it had experienced during the preliminary trials which Mr. Balzer had made sometime previous, a record of which he sent me, and a copy of his letter having been transmitted to the Secretary in my communication of August 4, 1899.

The combustion chamber and sides of the cylinder showed no effects of heating whatever, and Mr. Balzer stated that they did not become seriously heated during the run.

Mr. Balzer proposes to arrange a kind of "oil feed" so that the pistons, connecting rod bearing, crankshaft, and in fact all parts requiring lubrication will be oiled from one point. He will do this by making a small "oil vein" which he will place on the inner side of the drum, and which will lead to all parts requiring oil.

Mr. Balzer states that the engine in its present shape weighs 103 lbs. However the hollow shaft which is part of the flange of the supporting drum is about 8 in. longer than it need be so far as Mr. Balzer's contract is concerned.

Mr. Balzer again emphasized his financial difficulties and the consequent delay of the completion of the engine on this account. However, I will not go into this as a complete summary of the matter is given in my letter of August 22, 1899 to Mr. Rathbun, also in my letter of August 25th to the Secretary, and of the same date to Mr. Rathbun "Q.V."

As there was very little time to be lost I told Mr. Balzer to meet me

---

[24] A device for ascertaining horsepower consisting of a band brake attached to a wheel driven by the engine being tested. The braking force is measured by a scale from which the engine's torque can be ascertained. The revolutions per minute of the engine is also determined. From these two variables the horsepower can be derived. See Figure 24.

early the next morning at my hotel, and I would go with him to see Mr. John W. Weed, 62 William Street, New York about the furnishing of a bond to secure a second advance of $500 on the contract price of $1,500 for the engine, I advising such an advance to be made.

On August 22nd I spent the morning with Mr. Balzer in going to see Mr. Weed about the furnishing of a bond and getting the matter arranged by one o'clock. I then took Mr. Balzer to lunch. After which he went back to Mr. Weed's office to sign the bond and forward it to Mr. Rathbun that evening.

On August 23rd I again went out to Mr. Balzer's in the early morning, and found the engine in running condition before I reached there. On my arrival Mr. Balzer started up the engine, which he stated had been running a short while before, and the one cylinder which had been fitted up worked very nicely under the circumstances. The compression as shown by the gauge attached to the combustion chamber was 60 lbs. per sq. in. *regularly*. The explosions were 110 per minute, and varied all the way from about 120 lbs. clean up to more than 240, the gauge reading to only 200 lbs., but the needle being thrown clear around at times until it struck the guard pin at the zero mark, and on one or two occasions the needle was bent very severely. I was unable to make a brake test, as the Prony brake was not in shape, but from what I saw I feel very much encouraged, and am rather inclined to believe that the one cylinder will develop 4 hp., and if this is the case the 5 cylinders ought to develop more than 20 hp. allowing for the power which will be consumed in the rotation of the cylinders, and the resistance to be overcome on account of this rotation, and the added resistance of the radiating ribs.

The head of the cylinder, however, heated up so in about 5 minutes that premature explosion occurred unless some waste which had been soaked in water was shoved between the head of the cylinder and the flange of the supporting bearings. As soon as this dampened waste was pressed against the head of the cylinder the premature explosion was practically overcome; however, the water evaporated very quickly, and the waste had to be continually wetted. As to whether the radiating ribs which Mr. Balzer proposes to place on the head of the cylinder will keep it cool or not, I confess I am unable to say, but I feel that it is best at any rate to complete the engine as at present planned as we can tell nothing about what will happen until it is completed and tried, and as there remains now very little to be done, I consider it on the whole, without question [advisable] to complete it immediately and try it.

I am going to have Mr. Balzer send on the remaining parts of the

49

"second engine" which is now lying over in the National Museum, and expect to put it in working shape, and attach one of the large 2½ ft. propellers to it, and drive the propeller around, and if possible, determine the thrust, and knowing the thrust, and number of revolutions I can very readily determine the horsepower expended, and from this I will be able to calculate very closely as to what the propellers will do when used on the great aerodrome.[25] I will have him send the parts immediately so that I can, if possible, make this test before the Secretary returns. This engine is capable of developing about 2½ or 3 hp., and will I think do very nicely for the work I wish to employ it in.

I left Mr. Balzer with the understanding that I would see that $500 of the contract price was advanced to him immediately, and that he would spare no effort to push the work forward, so that if possible the engine would be completed and ready for trial before the Secretary returns. Mr. Balzer stated that he would certainly have it finished in two weeks. However, Mr. Balzer has been promising the engine *"next week"* every week for the last five months, but I am inclined to believe that [although] we may expect to find that he may not be able to keep the cylinders cool we will have it here at work before the close of next month.

12 September 1899—Manly to Langley in Washington, D.C. (in part)

The engine for the great aerodrome is as yet unfinished, but Mr. Balzer promises to be ready with it by the 22nd of the present month, *at the very outside.* In order to use the engine on the great aerodrome, provision will have to be made for supporting it and attaching it to the frame, and Mr. Balzer was expected to have made these supports while he was constructing the traverse frame last spring. However, it was not done then, although I gave Mr. Balzer instructions as to how I wished the work executed, and he promised me on my last visit to him on August 21, 1899, that he would put some extra men at work on these supports and complete them immediately.

It will also be necessary to have made a clutch, by means of which the engine can be started up under "no load," and when it has gotten up its speed, the load can then be thrown on by means of a clutch. Mr. Balzer is now at work on this clutch, and will, I think, have it completed and ready for delivery with the engine.

It will be necessary to provide two sets of bevel gears of about 3 in. or 4 in. diameter, and 8 pitch, to be used in transmitting the power from the engine to the shafting, which in turn transmits it to the propellers.

---

[25] This refers to the spare engine which came with Balzer's quadricycle of 1894.

These gears had better be provided by Mr. Balzer, who will turn up the blanks for them, and send them to Bilgram, of Philadelphia, to be cut.

Before the engines can be used on the aerodrome, a specially light carbureter, of a capacity of about three gallons, will have to be made, and this had also best be done by Mr. Balzer.

21 September 1899—Manly in Washington, D.C. (quoting from Balzer's letter) to Langley in Boston

Yours of the 12th received, and in reply to the same would say that I have been so busy that I have been unable to give the carbureters any time. I have found that my first idea of the wick system would not work.

Please find enclosed a rough sketch of one with which I have been partly successful, and which I intend to use on your engine.

The work on the engine is progressing slowly, as we have had a great deal of trouble in bending the tubes of the feed and exhaust pipes. We now have all the valves set on the engine, and we are finishing up the spark mechanism and the lubricating channels, and I expect no later than Saturday, to give you a full report of the working of the engine with five cylinders.

26 September 1899—Balzer in New York City to Langley in Washington, D.C. Langley was in Boston, and Manly forwarded the letter

Your telegram of today, to Mr. Weed, has been handed over to me, and in reply would say that I have had the engine running with five cylinders, and after running for sometime the crankshaft froze tight, making it necessary to take the engine apart and replace the brasses which we are doing now with most possible haste. It is very difficult to get the proper mechanics, at the present time, to do this work, as New York is turned up-side down on account of Dewey's Day.[26]

I am personally at this work, and if things run smoothly, I will have the lubricating cups and all accessories to the engine finished by Thursday, the 28th, but as Friday and Saturday are two holidays I will be unable to get any one to do the work.

All parts of the engine work satisfactory, and as for the horse power, I cannot give you that until I have had the engine run fully a day, or so as to run the piston rings and the cylinders down smoothly, as we dare

---

[26] It will be recalled that Mr. Weed was Balzer's bondsman. Manly had sent him a telegram to put pressure on Balzer. This is an important date as it marks the first time the engine was run in its entirety. Dewey's Day was 30 September 1909.

not use any emery in fear of cutting them. I will also advise you of the progress of the engine tomorrow at the same time.

3 October 1899—Waste book entry by Manly (in part)

I left Washington on Tuesday afternoon for New York arriving there that evening, and the next morning went out to see Balzer. I found him at work on the engine assisted by 5 or 6 men, and he was then finishing up some of the parts for the valves of the engine.

I spent the day with Balzer going over the work on the engine, and laying out designs for the bed-plates for supporting it. These bed-plates are to be so made that in case it becomes necessary to have another engine, both engines can be very easily held within the present frame without any very serious changes being made.

I called on the Secretary at 4:30 o'clock in the afternoon at the Metropolitan Club, and laid before him very plainly the conditions of the work.

8 October 1899—Waste book entry by Manly

I met Mr. Balzer at 7:25 this morning at the station and after taking him to breakfast went immediately to the Institution where we have been at work talking over the question of the engine, frame work, etc.

I have also taken Balzer out to the South Shed so that he may see the traverse frame again and get it clearly fixed in his mind.

About 11 o'clock the Secretary arrived at the building, and after discussing the matter with him and informing him of Mr. Balzer's visit, I have been able to get him to come to a definite conclusion about the matter, and to write me a letter authorizing me to give the work to Mr. Balzer under contract.

I have given Balzer drawings of the bed-plates, bearings, supports for bearings, etc., and he left this afternoon at 4 o'clock.

13 October 1899—Telegram from Langley in Washington, D.C., to Balzer in New York City

I find that it will be necessary to have the engine, even in its uncompleted state, in Washington by October 17th, and I desire therefore, that you will ship it so that it may reach here by that time.

I am also desirous of seeing you here at the time that the engine is sent on, and if you can come here on the evening of October 16th, and remain a day or so, I will be very glad to have you reimbursed for the expenses incurred for your travel and subsistence on account of this visit.

14 October 1899—Telegram from Balzer in New York City to Manly in Washington, D.C.

Your telegram received this noon. I will ship all the parts of the engine Monday noon, and will follow myself on the 4 o'clock train but will be unable to have the engine complete by that time. I am doing the best I can.

17 October 1899—Waste book entry by Manly (in part)

I met Mr. Balzer at the depot last night at 8:30, and spent the evening with him discussing the engine, bed-plates, etc., going over the question of the radiating cooling fins ribs, the proportion that their thickness should bear to the thickness of the cylinder walls of the engine.

Balzer has about finished up the engine; the only things remaining now to be done are to finish up some of the valve rods for the feed and the exhaust connections, and to make preliminary runs until he can get the cylinders properly worked in. This will probably require a week or so more. I think the whole thing would have been completed ready for a short run by October 24 had the Board not changed the date of their inspection.

The engine, bed-plates, etc., were shipped at noon yesterday by Mr. Balzer, and will therefore probably arrive in Washington this morning. As soon as they arrive they will be placed in their proper position in the traverse frame and the whole ready to be turned over by hand.

The engine, bed-plates, etc., arrived by express at 11 o'clock, and were immediately placed in the frame. I have been busy with Mr. Balzer all day.

19 October 1899—Waste book entry by Manly

While talking with Mr. Balzer I brought up the question of the building of a small engine of about 1½ horse power for use on the proposed new and larger model of the great aerodrome. Balzer thinks the engine can probably be built for about 12 lbs. weight, but is unwilling to accept contract for such an engine, and in fact, will not undertake the engine under any circumstances until the large engine is completed.

I have today been again discussing with the Secretary the question of the probability of having Balzer build the 1½ hp. gasoline engine for the new model of the great aerodrome, and the Secretary is very desirous of securing the engine, and if the engine is successful, will certainly have the new model built.[27]

---

[27] This model gasoline aero engine is in the National Aeronautical Collection.

53

The Secretary has also had Balzer look over the sketch of his apparatus for controlling the movements of the Penaud rudder, and Balzer agrees to make a rough working drawing of the same, the drawing to indicate the general method to be pursued in making a model of it.

The engine, bed-plates, etc., were today boxed so that they may be returned to Balzer tomorrow for completion. Balzer left this afternoon at 4 o'clock, it being now certain that the Board of O[rdnance] and F[ortification] will make no inspection for the present.

1 November 1899—Waste book entry by Manly

The model of the device for securing automatic equilibrium in the great aerodrome was received from Balzer today. Balzer, however, misunderstood the directions of the Secretary with reference to it, and the model is consequently not what was desired. I expect to draw out in detail the plans for this apparatus, and will construct it here, as it will require constant supervision while it is being made.[28]

15 November 1899—Balzer in New York City to Manly in Washington, D.C. (in part)

This is the first chance that I have had to dictate a letter and report on the progress of the engine since I left you three weeks ago.

One of the "I" beams of the engine, as I have written you, buckled up and had to be replaced with a new one, but the tubing that I telegraphed for yesterday was a mistake on my part. Instead of making one of the supports in the center and the other $3\frac{1}{4}$ in. from the center, I made them both alike.

There has been a great deal of detail work on the engine, small and no end of fitting, but now we have the engine complete with five cylinders, all connections made, and the starting bar finished, but have not had any time to put on the attachment to throw the spark ahead, that is, shifting the ignition cam, of which I spoke to you. The inlet of the engine is $1\frac{1}{8}$ in. pipe, but I do not know at what angle you want the pipes to lead, yet I have so arranged them that you can put them in any position. The connecting rods and gears are all hardened and ground, but I have still to make the carbureter, the tank and the moving device of the igniting cam.

I am going to give the engine a test tomorrow morning, with the five cylinders working complete, and will report the result to you tomorrow —that is give you the speed, horse power and time of premature explosion if any. For this test I will use the wagon tank, and if the time

---

[28] This early autopilot was built but not tested.

54

should be so short that I will not be able to make a new tank for you and [a new] carbureter, I would advise you to use this [the wagon carbureter] and I will bring it on. I think that we can make a satisfactory test of it.

I trust that you have completely recovered from your cold which you had when I was down there, and hope that you are feeling better than I, for I am simply over-worked trying to get this work out.

20 November 1899—Waste book entry by Manly

I met Mr. Balzer at the depot last night at 8:30 o'clock and went with him to his hotel. We spent the evening discussing the possible improvements in the engine.

This morning Mr. Balzer came down to the building at 9 o'clock and went to the South Shed to get things ready for the engine which arrived about 11 o'clock. The carbureter, however, did not come, although it was shipped at the same time as the engine, and I have sent George Wells over to the Express (Adams) Office to see that proper steps are taken to have it here by tomorrow morning.

The engine is, so far as mechanical construction is concerned, practically complete with the exception of the oiling ring with the special aluminum cup, which is to be used for keeping the crank shaft, pistons, etc., properly lubricated, the "cam" for varying the time of ignition, the possibly necessary radiating ribs on the ends of the cylinders, and the carbureter. The carbureter which Balzer had sent on but which had not yet arrived, was one belonging to one of his automobiles, and is too small for supplying sufficient gas when the engine is run to its maximum power.

21 November 1899—Waste book entry by Manly (in part; refers to an inspection by the Board of Ordnance and Fortification)

Judge Outhwaite, Captain Lewis, Capt. Wheeler, Capt. Davis, Mr. Bell, and Mr. Walcott called at the Institution building at 2:30 o'clock, and after a short talk with the Secretary came out to the South Shed to look over the progress of the aerodromic work. After spending about an hour at the South Shed appearing very much interested and pleased at the progress of the work and at the intricacy of the problems connected with it, they all with the exception of Mr. Walcott went to the house boat at the 8th Street Wharf to see it. They were there shown No. 5 with its wings, rudder, etc. mounted, and also the working of the lower launching apparatus.

After inspecting the inside of the boat, they all went on top to see the turntable, etc., after which they departed.

21 November 1899—Wells diary, (in part; same event as above)

They appeared to be very much pleased with the condition of things, and especially with the engine. Balzer receiving the congratulations of the party for turning out such a magnificent piece of work.

Owing to the failure of the Express Company to deliver the carbureter, the engine could not be run by gasoline, but was turned over by hand, which seemed to be sufficient for the occasion.

23 November 1899—Memorandum from Langley to Manly

You know my extreme desire to have a brake horse test of Mr. Balzer's engine, now here.

I understand from Mr. Balzer that the following things are to be made before this can be properly done:

1. A carbureter and copper tank. (This represents about a week's work.)
2. The sparking device (which is within about 3 days of being finished.)
3. The special aluminum oil cup which will oil all five cylinders at once.
4. The starting device.

Mr. Balzer thinks that with good fortune he may have these ready in a fortnight.

With the above four things the engine will be entirely ready to turn; but before the horsepower test is made, it ought to be run (Mr. Balzer says) 3 or 4 days under the eye of the maker, to be sure that the cylinders will not cut. While it is running, the maker can determine whether there is danger of premature explosion from overheating, and whether it will be necessary to put on the radiating ends (which may take a week more time).

You will please see that everything is ready for the brake tests before the close of next week. This includes the strengthening of the tubes in the aerodrome frame immediately about the engine, so that it may be tested in the frame itself. The completion of the heavy rolling carriage [29] on which the whole frame is to be mounted during the test, the providing space for doing this while carrying the wheels [propellers], the provision of a suitable single Prony brake (which Mr. Balzer is ready to take the risk of applying to one side of his engine only, with the whole of the power), the provision of the requisite apparatus for testing the thrust and, at the same time, testing the speed of the propellers, I desire that all the above shall be, as far as possible rehearsed; that

---

[29] This is a device to measure static propeller thrust.

is to say, the frame actually mounted in place; the wheels [propellers] put on and actually turned, if only by hand; and every portion so that it will be sure that everything is there and ready in its proper position.

3 January 1900—Telegram from Manly in New York City to Langley in Washington, D.C.

Arrived last evening at Balzer's shop. Now he has had engine running light up to eight hundred revolutions without overheating, but sparking device must be slightly changed before brake test can be made. Will make test tomorrow.

4 January 1900—Telegram from Manly in New York City to Langley in D.C.

Have had shop running until eight tonight. Will certainly make test by noon tomorrow. Arrive Washington Friday evening.

10 January 1900—Manly in Washington, D.C., to Balzer in New York City

I have arranged to have a further advance of $400 made to you and the check with the accompanying letter will be mailed tomorrow.

I have had to practically guarantee this amount myself and further assure the Secretary that the engine will be ready for its official test by the third of February.

Now pray don't disappoint me in this matter as I have staked a great deal on your being certain to allow nothing to interfere with the completion of the engine by February 3rd.

I will send the pieces of tubing to you by mail tomorrow.

Please send me that $1/16$ in. roller that you used in the construction of the bedplates for the engine. I mean the one for grooving the tubing. I enclose a franked and addressed envelope in which you can enclose it.

By the way, I find I will have to hasten things here at double speed and am going to double my force. However, I can guarantee a man for only three months work, though I may need one longer. Do you think that the man you spoke of would like to come under these conditions at $3.00 per day with hours from 8 a.m. to 4 p.m., and full pay for legal holidays. If he cares to come please let me know with his name and initials by return mail, as I expect to fill all of the places by the close of this week.

12 January 1900—Langely in Washington, D.C., to Balzer in New York City

Referring to your oral request, made through Mr. Manly on his last visit of inspection of the condition of the gasoline engine, that owing to the number of changes which had proved necessary in the engine, and to the additional expense incurred thereby, you be advanced $400 more of the contract price of $1,500 for the engine, making $1,400 in all of this contract price which has been advanced, I desire to say that owing to the extreme urgency of the matter, I will authorize that a further advance of $400 of the contract price be made you, upon condition that you will allow nothing to interfere with the immediate completion of the engine.

Mr. Manly informs me that as a result of the recent preliminary trials which you have made on the engine, it has been found that it will not be necessary to add the radiating ribs on the heads of the cylinders and the explosion chambers, in order to prevent premature explosion, as you have so far had no trouble on this point. I am gratified to learn this, but regret that the procuring of a suitable sparking arrangement has caused so much experiment and consumed so much time, thus causing a very serious delay. However, I trust that with this additional advance which I now authorize, you will spare no effort to complete the engine at the earliest possible date, allowing no outside work to interfere with it, and that you will certainly have the engine in Washington for its official trial by the 3rd of February.

15 January 1900—Memorandum by Manly to Langley (in part)

CONDITION OF AERODROMIC WORK ON DECEMBER 31, 1899

Mr. Balzer has completed all of the different parts and has assembled it and had it running light on two or three occasions, but has each time found troubles existing in the sparking arrangement which have demanded the dismounting of the engine, and the design and construction of suitable variations in the sparking arrangement. The difficulties which have been met in the sparking arrangement have not existed in the mere contact points, but have arisen with what is known as the "spark shifter," a device which must so control the spark as to enable the operator to cause the explosion at any designated point of the stroke. This is absolutely necessary, as the engine upon first starting up must be exploded just after the cylinder [piston] passes the dead center, whereas the point of explosion is gradually made to occur earlier in the stroke as the speed goes up until, running at about 500 or 600 revolutions, the proper time of explosion is found to be at a point about 30° before the cylinder [piston] reaches its dead center. However, it is encouraging to be able to state that Mr. Balzer has now found a very ingenious shifting device which I think will, after a few slight changes, prove entirely suitable for the present case, and I am now encouraged to think that the engine will not only fulfill its contract, but perhaps under favorable circumstances show as much as 18 to 20 brake horsepower.

The greatest difficulty in the way of immediate completion of the engine is the fact that Mr. Balzer who has already expended two or three times the contract price of the engine in its construction, has practically no means, outside of a small income required for personal living expenses, at his disposal for carrying on the work.

4 February 1900—Balzer in New York City to Manly in Washington, D.C.

Your cable received—would say that you can depend on twenty horsepower at 500 rev., and I will ship engine about Thursday this week. Wright will report to you tomorrow and I will send you another man about the middle of the month. Will write tomorrow.

5 February 1900—Wells diary (in part)

F. F. Wright, formerly with Balzer in N.Y.C. as a machinist, reported here for work this morning.

14 February 1900—Langley in Washington, D.C., to Balzer in New York City

Mr. Manly has communicated to me your letter of the 13th which is just received. I am sorry to hear that you have had trouble with the ball-joint of the connecting rod, but am prepared by what Mr. Manly tells me not to feel surprised that you have found it necessary to run the exhaust pipes around the carbureter.[30]

Please send the other mechanic you speak of, on the same terms which I have offered Wright, and if you know of still another please send him also.

Please be good enough to write me by Saturday or Sunday what progress you have made with the engine since your letter of the 13th to Mr. Manly.

19 February 1900—Wells diary

Austin H. Philbrook, a machinist from Balzer, reports for duty this morning and is set to work in Stable Shop with Wright, another of Balzer's men. He is to receive $3.25 per day.

---

[30] The piston was joined to the connecting rod by a ball and socket joint in contrast to the modern practice of using a piston pin. Apparently it had been necessary to "run the exhaust pipes around the carbureter" in order to increase the vaporization of the fuel.

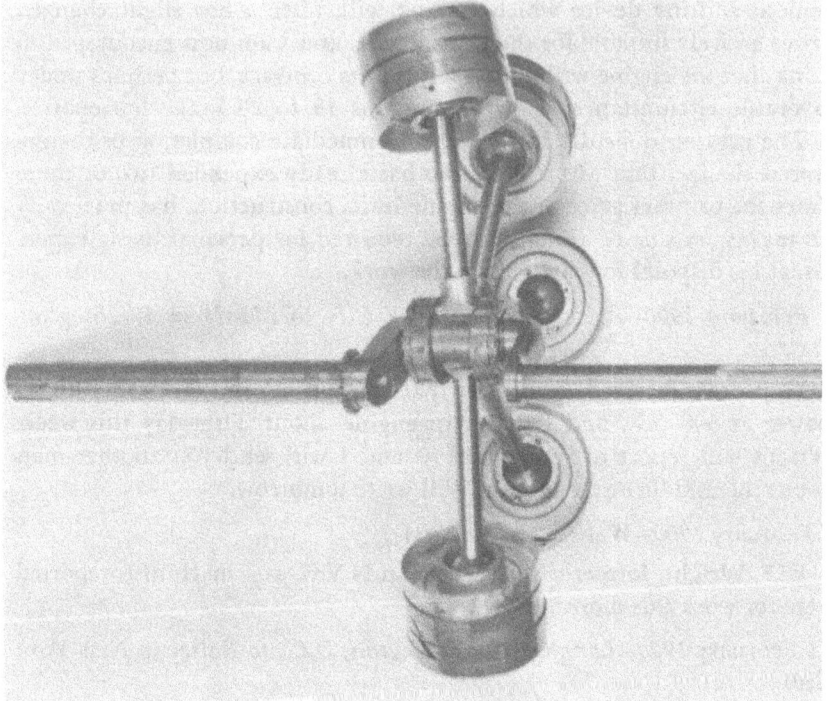

FIGURE 18.—Crankshaft, connecting rods, and pistons assembly from Langley's model aero engine illustrating slipper crankshaft and ball joint piston bearings as used in the original version of the full size engine. Now on exhibit at the Smithsonian Institution. (Smithsonian photo A-4425.)

20 February 1900—Langley to Wells both in Washington, D.C.

I take pleasure in informing you that, in recognition of your efficient services, your compensation has been fixed at the rate of $60.00 a month, beginning February 15, 1900.

5 March 1900—Wells diary

G. D. MacDonald and R. S. Newham, two machinists procured from Balzer in New York by Mr. Manly last week, report for work this morning.

MacDonald put at work in upper laboratory, and Newham in stable shop.

20 March 1900—Manly in Washington, D.C., to Balzer in New York City (in part)

The Secretary realizes the difficulties under which you have been working, and the great amount of reconstruction of parts of the work that you have had to do, and he thoroughly appreciates the spirit in which you have met all the difficulties, his appreciation having been shown by the way in which he set aside precedent and rule in doing all that was possible for him to do in a financial way. However, you must realize that it is nothing but natural that he is now very uneasy concerning the ultimate success of the large engine, the entire machine for which it was intended being now about complete, and having consumed not only thousands of dollars, but also a large portion for the last two years of his available time from his multitudinous official duties. This will be made more clear to you when you note the fact that the entire frame work which you have seen, will be entirely worthless should it become necessary to undertake the construction of a different type of engine which would necessarily mean the entire change of design and reconstruction of all this frame work, and such a reconstruction would inevitably mean a further delay for many months and the expenditure of several thousands of dollars.

As I have said to you during conversation recently, the Secretary stands ready to not only give you all credit for your part in the work and to insure this will be properly recognized by the public generally, but will, I am certain, recognize your success in a pecuniary way.

Now I must say in a personal way, and I think you will agree with me, that there is no one who more thoroughly recognized the difficulties with which you have had to contend, or who more thoroughly appreciates the difficulty of the work which you have undertaken, and I have at all times done my best to render you all assistance possible. Our relations from the very beginning of the work have been of the most pleasant nature, and at no time has there been any change in this relation, and I hope and expect that there will never be any occasion which would cause such a change. However, you must realize that there is a limit to the number of times that a man of the Secretary's experience will allow himself to be given assurance that everything is progressing as well as possible, and then after waiting several months, things are in practically no better shape than they were before, without losing confidence in the person giving him such assurance, and I fear that unless this large engine is completed very soon that it may be the means of the Secretary losing all confidence in my judgment and advice.

I hope you understand the matter as I have tried to explain it to you, and will do all in your power to see that such a state of affairs as I have last mentioned will have no reason to arise.

Referring to the terms of my contract with Mr. Balzer, to your letter of April 4th, to my visit to Mr. Balzer yesterday, and to the doubt which we both feel whether he will deliver this week the engine fulfilling even the terms of the contract (not to speak of the greatly higher power which we anticipated), I feel that the matter is serious and that I shall have to decide finally this week what expedient to adopt. I do not forget that from the beginning I have reckoned, as in my letter of June 21, 1898, on using two engines developing from 10 to 12 horsepower each at a weight of 100 pounds apiece. If Balzer's engine then gave only 10 brake horsepower for 100 lbs., he would still be doing what I first expected as the largest probable achievement in this direction, but his engine has now been delayed over a year with experiments on experiments, and in that year we might have constructed the engine if we had known nothing better was to be had.

I understand it to be your belief that most of the difficulties are introduced by making the engine itself revolve so as to be its own fly-wheel, and that you think it might give very much more than the 12 horsepower contracted for if the question of weight did not enter in, and if the engine did not revolve, but had a fly-wheel to help it pass dead center. I have suggested as worth trying a small light fly-wheel, giving it a very high rate of speed.

The second difficulty, of course, is the cooling of the cylinders when they are not revolving. This would be a matter for subsequent consideration. If we could run them for fifteen minutes surrounded with a wet cloth or some such device for momentary action, we could in that time do everything that might be necessary to insure the success of the test, which has never been definitely put, but which I will suppose to be the carrying of a man something like a mile in two or three minutes, returning to the start in safety. To provide a new rotating engine at a high cost will involve waiting at least ten weeks or more, and an expenditure, I suppose, at a minimum of $1,500, but probably much more. Please give me your opinion on the advisability of experimenting on a stationary engine with a small fly-wheel. If neither of the plans

---

[31] This memorandum marked the beginning of a loss of faith in Balzer and the rotary engine by Langley and Manly. From this point onward, Manly's influence with Langley increased and he became fully responsible for the engine's development. A trip to Europe shortly afterwards convinced both Langley and Manly that rotary engines were not practical. Therefore, upon Manly's return, he converted the engine from a rotary to a static radial in which form its evolution continued.

work, the gas engine seems to be condemned. It is to be hoped then that one or the other of them will do.

I will still hope that Balzer's engine will arrive next week, developing more than the contracted horsepower, but if it does not, I have come·to a crucial point where I must finally take one of the different roads that open, the least desirable of all being the adoption of the steam engine instead of the gas engine. I cannot bring myself to contemplate this last possibility.

I desire that you will take everything that I have said into consideration, and shall be pleased to have you express your own opinion as to what is to be done if Balzer's promise is broken, as so many of his promises have been.

12 April 1900—Balzer in New York City to Langley in Washington, D.C. (in part)

Replying to Assistant Secretary Mr. Rathbun's letter of the 11th, I regret very much to say that I was unable to ship the large engine to you on Tuesday as I promised, as I have been unable to get the proper material in time to finish the same. Also I have discovered since your visit, that the connecting rods must be re-hardened.

When I made the promise to ship the engine to you I was in hopes of getting the proper workmen to help me out, but I have been unable to secure men who do accurate and fine work as they are now scarce. And while we are making all efforts by working over time, it is almost impossible for me to have any work done by the men, unless I help them by giving my personal attention, and this I am doing. The men when alone are simply afraid that the work is too light, therefore progress is very slow.

Mr. Manly asked me over the telephone if the engines could be operated by revolving the cylinders, and also by revolving the crankshaft: This can be done without injury to any parts as they are strong enough to stand the strain, but the engines will run steadier if the cylinders are revolved.

9 May 1900—Langley to Manly both in New York City

After calling with you on Balzer this morning and finding that there are neither efficient preparations made for the brake test, nor that any can be made within two days, I have decided that you must stay here til they are made, and desire that you will see that they are made with the greatest possible dispatch. I wish at least three different speeds tested, and something definite ascertained. Balzer may work his force over time, if necessary, in putting in bushings where the thing has heated, or in other ways, and you, if you judge fit, may pay him for his men's over time, or for the outside work, to the extent of $100.

I am going to leave town for Washington tomorrow, and hope to see you after another interview with Balzer, bringing him down with you to this hotel at half past five this afternoon.

11 May 1900—Langley in Washington, D.C., to Balzer in New York City (in part)

Referring to my visit to your shop on Wednesday, the 9th instant, I desire that you will construct immediately the wheels and brakes necessary for a Prony brake trial of the large engine.

I will meet the necessary expenses connected with this construction so that the brakes may be brought on and kept permanently here.

15 May 1900—Wells diary

The Secretary telegraphs to Mr. Manly instructing him not to leave until he receives letter from Secretary.

Secretary writes to Mr. Manly asking for final report on engines which will decide the Secretary as to whether he will throw Balzer over or not.

The Secretary calls Mr. Manly up on long distance telephone this afternoon about 2:20 in regard to work on engines.

The Secretary receives a letter from Mr. Manly in New York today stating that he had made three brake tests of the large engine, each one being very unsatisfactory as regards the hp. obtained.

Discusses difficulties in way of engine reaching requisite hp. Will procure a new carbureter and make another trial tomorrow morning. Though, if he is unable to procure carbureter, he will leave New York for Washington this afternoon at 3:25 unless he hears from the Secretary to the contrary by telegraph.

19 May 1900—Wells diary

The Secretary receives a letter from Mr. Manly today dated the 18th, and acknowledges the Secretary's letter of the 16th. Expected to make a test of large engine by today and another test Monday. Mr. Manly says that it is his firm conviction that Balzer's engine offers more chance of success for purposes intended than any other plan of construction with which he is acquainted. Thinks that minor faults in engine which prevents good results in hp. tests will be overcome very shortly.

19 May 1900—Langley in Washington, D.C., to Manly in New York City (in part)

I received your interesting letter of the 18th this morning. I desire that you will still remain, at any inconvenience to the work here, until you can advise me certainly as to the performance of the engine under the brake meeting the requirements (I mean the requirements as to horse power; for those as to time and other conditions, concessions might be made upon).

I have never doubted, after the careful examination you first gave it, that the non-success of the engine was not due to faulty mechanical or thermodynamic principles. At the same time I believe I mentioned that I was warned by people of experience that the combination of minor difficulties, such as cannot be forecast or certainly overcome, has hitherto prevented entire success with any gas engine at all; at least with one so light as I am trying for.

Now I cannot contemplate continuing these experiments indefinitely or in your absence. You must stay then, until you get something definite one way or the other; or if you do not see your way to getting something definite (I mean a satisfactory brake test), that itself is a conclusion.

I do not want you to be hampered by lack of money. I sent you, on May 11th, $100; I sent Balzer $300 through your hands; and am sending you tonight $100 more. You understand, and Balzer will understand, that I have got no more to send until I get news that the engine has fulfilled its contract, at least the horse power part, without reference to time and other conditions; and that as soon as this is done I can ask the Ordnance Board to grant more money, and will if you recommend it.

20 May 1900—Wells diary

The Secretary receives a special delivery letter this morning from Mr. Manly in New York in regard to work on large engine, dated the 19th (Sat.).

States that he has made four more tests of large engine under different conditions from those of last Monday. Gives results of tests.

Engine developed approximately 8 hp. at 700 R.P.M. and 7½ hp. at 500 R.P.M. Says will work on engine today at shops.

Says results of tests are to him (C.M.M.[anly]) very encouraging. Everything possible being done to expedite work.

21 May 1900—Wells diary

A telegram received from Manly at 3 o'clock this p.m. "Men have quit work on account of inability to pay back wages. Recommend Wright, Philbrook, and Newham be sent on tonight and kept on our pay roll rest of month. Answer."

The Secretary approves this recommendation of Mr. Manly's and has G. B. Wells notify men mentioned to leave 10 o'clock tonight for New York and report to Balzer's shop first thing in the morning. Furnished transportation orders for the three men to New York. Also advances $5.00 to get their breakfasts in New York and pay car fare to Balzer's shop where they will meet Mr. Manly.

G. B. Wells notifies Mr. Manly by telegraph of Secretary's approval of recommendation.

24 May 1900—Wells diary

The Secretary receives a letter from Mr. Manly this morning stating that he fears engine tests will not be made until Friday on account of delay caused by making new piston rings.

Speaks in regard to premature explosions of engine. If requisite power is not obtained Friday morning, corrections will be made, and further tests will be made Saturday or Sunday.

30 May 1900—Wells diary

The Secretary receives a private letter from Mr. Manly in regard to condition of things at Balzer's shops. Men refuse to work, etc. States that he has advanced Balzer money out of personal funds.

3 June 1900—Wells diary

The Secretary receives a special delivery letter from Mr. Manly this morning. Has had some very discouraging and exasperating delays in connection with anticipated test of Saturday, and expects to be busy all day Sunday with tests. Find that there is still some leakage.[32] This has been the most exasperating thing that has come up in the work.

States that if it were not for the large amount of delay which would be entailed by abandoning this gas engine to take up construction of different type of engine, he would not for one instant attempt to keep up the mental and physical strain which the work on Balzer's gas engine has been causing him.

The Secretary writes a personal note to Mr. Manly today cautioning him not to overtax himself in the work on the engine and sympathizing with him in regard to the way the work is going.

---

[32] Leakage was of compression around the contact points of the make and break ignition system.

Secretary receives letter from Mr. Manly today dated June 3, reporting that as a result of trial of Sunday, it is found that there is still much leakage of the compression around contact points, and that it will be necessary to construct some metal cups to fit around contact points. This will take about five days work, which he says will be undertaken rather than fail on some temporary arrangement.

Hopes that construction of steam engine will not be necessary.

Has made arrangements to procure three new machinists immediately, two taking the place of Wright and Philbrook and the third in the place the Secretary authorized in his letter of May 30. Will each receive $2.75 per day for his actual work. Gives account of money sent him while in New York.

13 June 1900—Manly in New York City to Langley in Washington, D.C.

It was past noon today before the first run could be made on the large engine, owing to the slipping of the contact rods (for the make and break ignition system) and consequently the necessary making of taper pins to hold these rods. However, at two o'clock everything being in readiness, the engine was started up. After only two turns by hand, it continued to revolve under its own power. Owing to some slight defect, however, it was found impossible to increase the speed above 400 revolutions per minute because of some trouble seeming to lay in the vibration of the brush which bears on the commutator and supplies the sparking current. During this test, however, it *steadily* maintained a pull of 30 lbs. on the 4' lever, running at a speed of 360 revolutions per minute, which is equivalent to 8 horse power.

Although this result was not as good as was expected, it was very encouraging, for although the engine in one of the previous trials pulled down only a slightly less number of pounds at a considerably greater speed, it did not do it regularly. That is, it did not maintain this power *continuously* in the previous trial. In this first test of today, however, the compression was perfect, though the exhaust gases were very black, indicating that the regulating valve [of the carbureter] was allowing too much gas and too little air to enter the combustion chambers. At the same time, the exhaust was *sharp and quick,* and it was the very irregular fluctuation in the sound of the exhaust, and the fact that the brush was seen to be sparking at the commutator, which led me to believe that the vibration of the brush was due to a certain amount of unavoidable shaking of the frame work, which caused the inability to increase the speed above 400 revolutions, *regardless of the load.*

If the engine had not heretofore on one occasion run at a speed as great as 600 or 700 revolutions per minute,[33] I would have thought it possible that the valves were incapable of working at such a high speed; but the fact that they had worked at this high speed previously made me look for some other cause. Heretofore there has been no trouble at the commutator, and this defect at present may be caused by the fact that in enlarging the sleeve, to allow the larger supply of gas to enter the engine, it was necessary to greatly increase the diameter of the commutator; and where there is a constant vibration in any running part, it also manifests itself to a very much greater degree as the diameter of the part is increased.

In order to make sure that the valves were working properly two more tests were made after the one above referred to, the stiffness of the springs on the valves being changed just previous to each of these tests. The results of both of these tests were practically the same as those noted, the exhaust remaining quick and sharp, the exhaust gases (though the [carbureter] regulating valve was turned to the limit of its adjustment) remaining black and dirty, and the report of the exhaust being still irregular at a speed as great as 350 revolutions, but becoming more uniform as the speed was reduced.

Immediately upon the completion of the last two tests, I started the men to work making a brush which will bear at three points of the commutator, and since the three arms of this brush will be of different periods of vibration, I hope that it will cure the trouble with the irregularity of the exhaust by insuring that at least one brush will always be bearing on the commutator. This brush will be completed in the morning, and I therefore expect to get several more tests during the course of the day.

It now seems that about all of the faults of construction have been remedied, and that it remains to endeavor to bring the engine up to the requisite power by making such changes in the adjustment of the different parts as the tests indicate to be necessary.

15 June 1900—Wells diary

The Secretary receives letter from Mr. Manly this morning dated the 14th. Stated that found this morning (the 14th) another special spark coil would be needed, and half a day spent in procuring a suitable one, one working at about 4,000 to 5,000 sparks per minute.

---

[33] But not under load.

Got two runs on engine late in afternoon, both rather unsatisfactory. Expects to change cams and valves to overcome minor difficulties. Expects to make further tests on the 15th.

15 June 1900—Langley in Washington, D.C., to Manly in New York City

I have your letter of the 14th and note what you say regarding the proposed further experimentation with a view to minimizing the amount of minor defects in the engine in the hope of obtaining the required horse power. I infer from it that the work is getting into the way which I apprehended it would and wrote about in my letter of May 19th. Please re-read that and you will see what I said about contemplating continuing these experiments indefinitely, and that while I wanted you to stay until you had a satisfactory brake test (I mean one developing the contract horsepower), that if you could not do that, that was in itself a conclusion.

We were then talking as if the matter would be settled in one way or another in a week or ten days, and I hope you felt and feel that I wanted to stand by you, but now each day has brought its new hope and its new failure in the way we know so well in the work here; until finally when you receive this, nearly six weeks of experiment will have elapsed, and (perhaps owing to my unfamiliarity with gas engines) I do not derive from what you say any absolute confidence that we are *materially* nearer a result than we were when you obtained 8 horsepower when first using the improved carbureter.

I have no question in my mind whatever, that you are doing all that it is possible for anyone in your position to do, and are working on this as if your own future were at stake with it. Do not misunderstand me then when I ask you, after re-reading our correspondence and remembering that it is impossible that I should continue this work indefinitely, if you can give me any positive assurance when the work will be done. I presume that you cannot, and that no man can.

I am leaving for Europe next week and I want to see you here before I go. I will therefore ask you to please come on next Monday at the latest, unless you prefer to be here Sunday. Telegraph early tomorrow.

Let me renew the advice given in my private letter of June 3rd, that you do not let the condition of things worry you, or over-tax your strength by trying to accomplish impossibilities before you return, and believe me.

382-902 O - 71 - 6

15 June 1900—Manly in New York City to Langley in Washington, D.C.

Four more tests of the engine were made today, the conditions prevailing in each test being somewhat varied each time. In the first test this morning, made at about 8 o'clock, the old cam was used, and a "rebound spring" was inserted back of the exhaust valve to make sure there was no sticking of the valve at the high rate of speed. The results of the test were practically the same as those of the previous one, of which I wrote you last night.

The second test was made just after noon, the old cam being replaced by the new one, the other conditions remaining practically the same. While the horsepower developed in this test was very little more than the 8 hp. procured in the test yesterday, the pull on the spring balance was very much more steady and uniform, the pointer varying at the maximum only about three or four pounds. The appearance of the heavy black smoke from the exhaust, while very much less than yesterday, was still observable. It was still found impossible, however, to raise the speed of the engine, even when running with no load, above 410 revolutions per minute, and the maximum power was again obtainable at the speed of 350 revolutions per minute.

The three or four tests were made under practically the same conditions as those prevailing in the second, except that the tension of the springs on the valves was increased each time, and the results obtained were practically the same.

If we assume a mean effective pressure of 70 lbs. per square inch (which is about what we would expect from a stationary engine of the same dimensions as this, that is $5\frac{1}{2}$ in. stroke by $4^3/_{16}$ in. diameter) and calculate what the *indicated* horse power would be at a speed of 350 revolutions per minute (which in the case of the present engine would mean 875 explosions per minute) we obtain as a result approximately 12 horse power; and multiplying this by the mechanical efficiency of 75 per cent, which is also about what we would expect in the present case, we obtain as a final result 9 brake horse power, which is very little more than the last tests have given.

Now, it is easily seen that if the valves can be made to work fast enough so that we obtain approximately the same mean effective pressure at a speed of about 530 revolutions per minute, we should get slightly over 12 horse power; and, of course, theoretically, the power to be obtained is only limited by the speed at which the valves will work without decreasing the mean effective pressure, the capacity of the inlet passages to convey sufficient gas in the short period of time in which they would have to act, and the danger of overheating due to an excessively large number of explosions within a limited time.

There are at present on each engine [cylinder] three valves, the first or main valve, which opens directly into the combustion chamber; second, the inlet valve opens into the sub-chamber and also communicates with the combustion chamber through the same main valve. The main valve is raised at the proper time by means of a cam, which is so geared that it makes 100 revolutions while the engine is making 400 (this ratio being due to the four cycles used), and the closing of the valve is caused by a spring which compels the roller, through which the main valve is actuated by the cam, to follow the "drop off" point and thus make the action of the valve independent of centrifugal force.

The exhaust and inlet valves are of the true "poppet" type, the inlet opening whenever there is a suction in the sub-chamber, and closing whenever there is pressure there; and the exhaust valve operating in exactly the reverse sense; that is, opening whenever there is a pressure, and closing whenever there is a suction in this sub-chamber. Now, it is easily seen that the exhaust and inlet valves are powerless to act unless the main valve is in its proper position, the main valve opening at the end of the stroke to allow the exhaust gases to be forced out on the return stroke, and remaining open until the engine has made one complete revolution, when it closes, the engine cylinder being then full of gases, since the back stroke of the engine forced the gases out and the second half of the revolution, or forward stroke, sucked the fresh gases in.

It is furthermore essential that this main valve should open at such a time as to cause the "point of release" to come at the proper place on the indicator diagram; that is, a small fractional part before the end of the stroke, and that it should close it exactly at the end of the suction stroke, so that none of the gases will be forced out through the exhaust valve when the piston starts to compress the charge preparatory to the next explosion.

I have dealt at some length with this matter of valves, since that is where the trouble now is; and I desire that you understand as far as possible the exact difficulties which I am attempting to overcome. It is possible that it may be necessary to put in a positive motion cam; that is one which will not only raise the main valve, but which will also jerk it down to its seat at the proper time, as it seems that the spring does not cause the roller, through which the main valve is actuated by the cam, to follow the contour of the cam at the opening and closing

71

CYLINDER & COMBUSTION CHAMBER
Large Balzer Engine

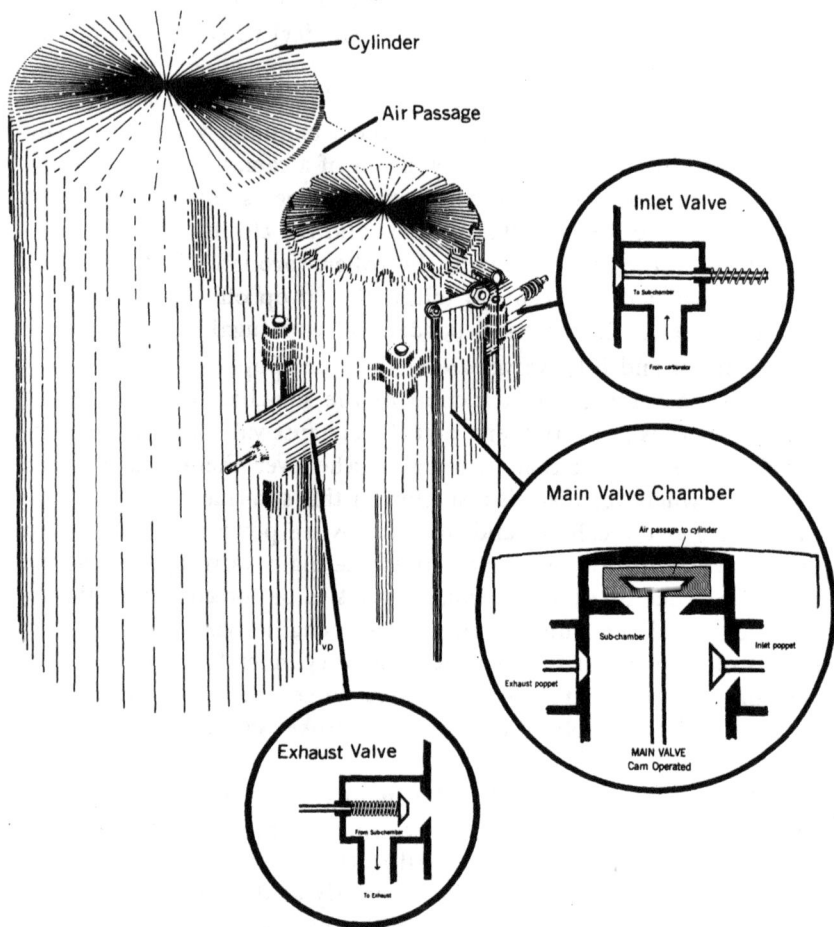

FIGURE 19.—Schematic drawing of valve system employed by Balzer. Drawing by Harry T. Hart (Smithsonian photo A4517.)

points.[34] Were it possible to make such a change as this in a day's time, I would, of course, not hesitate to do so; but as it may involve a delay of more than four or five days, I think it best to strive to overcome the difficulty in the way in which I am now experimenting, especially since,

[34] Manly is suggesting desmodromic valves such as used successfully by certain post-World War II Mercedes sports/racing cars.

as you know, that slight, but necessary changes are being made after each trial, and as suggested by such trials.

Your telegram with reference to the tubing was received this afternoon, and I will attend it.

19 June 1900—Manly to Langley both in Washington, D.C.

Referring to our conversation of this morning with reference to procuring a motive power for the great aerodrome, and in response to your oral request, I give the following brief statement of the present outlook in this direction.

The gasoline engine which was contracted for on the 12th of December, 1898 by Mr. Balzer can neither be accepted nor condemned at the present moment, since in the recent trials made upon it, it developed *steadily* and *regularly* 8 horsepower at 350 revolutions per minute with the valves working improperly, and while it cannot be accepted from the fact that it has not developed the 12 horsepower required, I do not think it best to condem it until it has been proven beyond question that no more power can be obtained from it even with the valves working as they should.

If there were a large number of defects in the mechanical principles employed in the construction of the engine, which would necessarily take an indefinite time to overcome and correct, I would of course recommend that work be immediately begun on a steam engine with its necessary boilers, condensers, burners, pumps, etc., but as this is not the case, and as I still believe most implicity that when the few defects now remaining, which prevent the proper amount of gases from entering the cylinders and being properly held there after they have exploded, have been corrected, that the engine will develop regularly and steadily a minimum of 12 horsepower.

I make this statement fully realizing that at present all manufacturers of gasoline engines are having more or less difficulty with their machines, but the very difficulties which these manufacturers are now having are the ones which have been entirely overcome in this engine during my recent visit in New York City, and I am firmly convinced that an engine suitable for the great aerodrome will be more quickly and surely procured by continuing the work on this present engine than by any other means, for the very defects which now remain are those which can be surely and certainly corrected.

While of course it is impossible for anyone to guarantee that the engine will be successful within a certain specified *time,* I desire to say that if it were a mere question of money loss instead of the much more

73

serious loss of *time,* I would not hesitate to stand accountable for any financial loss occasioned by continuing the attempts to correct the few faults now remaining in the engine. As I have said before, the engine has already cost Mr. Balzer more than $3,000 above the price which he will receive for it when it is complete, and of course all further experiments which he will make on it have been and will be a continual loss to him, but so great is his confidence in the engine, that he is determined to make it meet the requirements of the contract before he ceases work on it, and he will not abandon it even though the present contract with him be declared void.

In view of your wish that I go abroad for a few weeks to investigate all the different motors which may possibly afford some hope of being utilized for the great aerodrome, I recommend that Mr. Balzer be authorized to continue the work on the large engine, with the understanding that four machinists for this work will be carried on the O. and F. roll, and that they will at all times be kept employed making such changes in the details of construction, and that he be allowed to procure the materials for his work not to exceed the sum of one hundred ($100) dollars sending the vouchers here so that they may be paid in the regular way.

As forty days' time work of one man will complete all the work on the great aerodrome and its appurtenances that can be completed until my return, and as it is desirable that the present force of machinists be kept together if possible as they will all be needed when the engine does come, I recommend that McDonald and Newham, both of whom are good conscientious workmen, be sent to New York to work on the large engine, their names being continued on the O. and F. pay roll and they being used as two of the four men I have above recommended to work under the direction of Mr. Balzer. The two additional machinists of these four I can engage in New York City at a rate of $2.75 per day, there being two good men there now who have worked for me previously.

I may presume that I will be back within six weeks, and these recommendations are made on that assumption.

In regard to the one hundred dollars which I recommended be advanced Balzer for materials in connection with changes on the engine, I do not think that Balzer will need any money beyond this.

My reason for advising this advance to him is my belief that it is almost the one best thing to do in the interests of the Government. It is founded partly on my knowledge that he has spent nearly three thousand dollars on the engine outside the contract, and my absolute moral confidence that he will do the best he can to finish it in the next six weeks, and my belief that if it can be done by anyone it will be done by Mr. Balzer under these conditions.

20 June 1900—Langley to Manly both in Washington, D. C.

Referring to my conversation of this morning with you with reference to the engine which Mr. S. M. Balzer is now building for the great aerodrome, and to the necessity of immediately taking under consideration the procuring of some other motor for the aerodrome in case this engine of Mr. Balzer's fails there having already been a delay of more than fifteen months since the contract called for the completion of the engine, I desire that you go abroad on June 27th to make as thorough examination as possible of such light engines as are now being constructed in both England and on the Continent. I desire that you will proceed to New York City in time to have a consultation with Mr. Balzer on June 26th and to give him final directions as to the course of the work on the large engine during your absence, and that you take a passage for Europe on the "Germanic" sailing from New York for Liverpool on June 27th.

After examining the light engines in England, both gasoline and steam, you will proceed to France, going first to Paris and examining the engines there on exhibit and if necessary in any other cities in France. If time permits, you will visit Berlin, and if necessary, other cities in Germany which you may think advantageous, returning to Liverpool in time to take passage on the White Star Steamer "Cymric," sailing from that port on August 3rd.

Upon returning to New York City, you will investigate the progress which Mr. Balzer has made with the engine during your absence, and upon the completion of this duty you will return to Washington.

I desire that you take as copious notes as possible during these investigations, so that upon your return you may be able to give me a complete and definite report on the subject.

Your necessary expenses for travel and subsistence will be refunded to you upon the presentation of the proper vouchers therefor.

If in the course of the investigations you deem it necessary to employ the services of an interpreter, you are authorized to do so, and any such expenses will also be refunded to you.

25 June 1900—Manly in Washington, D.C., to Balzer in New York City (in part)

I will leave Washington at 12:45 Tuesday by way of the Penna. R.R. arriving at the 23rd Street Station at 6 p.m., and will go direct to the

Netherland Hotel. Please arrange to meet me at the hotel at 7:30 to dine with me.

Please make a rough sketch indicating what changes you think had best be made in the engine that can *certainly* be completed by four men, and the engine ready for trial again, within 30 days. I mean such changes as the making of new cylinder heads with new sub-chambers, the substitution of a positive motion cam, etc., so that we can discuss the matter very thoroughly Tuesday evening.

27 June 1900—Langley to Balzer both in New York City

Referring to the recent tests on the large engine in which the maximum power developed was 8 horsepower at 350 revolutions per minute, and to your conversation with Mr. Manly of June 26th, I desire that the two machinists McDonald and Newham, that I have just ordered to report to you at your shop, be put to work immediately under your direction on the construction of a five section commutator. This commutator should be so constructed and the brush which supplies the current so attached that the brush will be at all times shifted as the sparking lever is thrown the one way or the other.

As soon as this commutator is completed, the engine should be given a test to see whether the change has corrected the premature burning of the gases in the cylinder which now appears to occur at the moment, just preceding the compression stroke.

As it is possible that this five section commutator may not allow the contact points the proper rest, as soon as the test is completed and this point determined, and in case the desired rest is not secured, another section commutator revolving with the actuating gear and supplied from the second commutator revolving on the rotating cylinder should be built.

Upon the completion of these two changes in the engine and the proper tests as to the effect of the changes, and in case the engine still fails to come up to the required power the sub-chambers should be so arranged that the valve which is now the exhaust valve, will be made the inlet valve, and a new valve of larger dimensions made for the exhaust valve, and to be placed in the position which is now occupied by the inlet valve. When this change in the sub-chamber and valves is made, the inlet pipes which connect the sub-chamber and the rotating sleeve should be enlarged to at least $1\frac{3}{8}$ in. internal diameter ($1\frac{1}{2}$ in. being preferable if the space will allow). Upon the completion of this change in the valves and inlet pipes, a brake test of the engine should be made to determine the power developed.

As it will certainly be possible at times to expedite the work by working more than two men in the making of the changes mentioned, and in immediately completing the small engine along with the large one, you are authorized until further notice to employ two additional men at a rate not exceeding $3.00 per day, with the understanding that the compensation for their services will be obtained by your sending their time to the Disbursing Officer of the Institution who will enter their names on my pay-roll and forward the checks to you for their services at the proper period.

27 June 1900—Langley diary

Sailed from pier 48, North River, N.Y.C. at 12 o'clock today on "Germanic" for Liverpool, having C. M. Manly and G. B. Wells with me. S. P. L[angley] has stateroom 19, starboard side. C. M. Manly and G. B. Wells have berths in stateroom 62, port side. Weather very warm.

10 July 1900—Memorandum (in part) by Langley after a visit to H. S. Maxim, #18 Queen's Gate Place, London.

Mr. Maxim does not like the idea of the cylinders revolving on account of the difficulties it must necessitate in oiling and in sparking. Assuming that the Otto cycle is employed under ordinary conditions, a cylinder 3 inches in diameter and giving a 7 inch stroke, not only should but can and habitually does give 1,500 revolutions and 3 brake horsepower. An engine built by Count de Dion gives 3 brake horsepower at 1,500 revolutions, and 4 such cylinders would give 12 horsepower, and Mr. Maxim thinks it only a reasonable demand that they should be built for 100 lbs. weight. A smaller cylinder $2\frac{1}{4}$ inches in diameter, is in use by Mr. Walters, one of Maxim's employees, for an engine he has running a tricycle. The cylinder is $2\frac{1}{4}$ in. diameter and gives $2\frac{1}{4}$ brake horse. He did not dwell on the question of cooling except to say that if it were cooled directly by water, about $1/7$ the water for a steam engine would be needed. It is absolutely necessary that the speed should be more like 1,500 revolutions rather than 350, even 600 revolutions according to Mr. Maxim, would be most injudiciously slow. Everything otherwise depends on the judicious mixture of the gasses, and consequently on the carbureter as well as on the conditions of compression and the period in the cycle at which the spark is made.

11 July 1900—Langley in London to Manly in London (in part)

I repeat what I have said in our conversation, that whether the Balzer engine be or be not a failure, I desire that you will act in your visit here as though it was, and as though I must obtain a new gas engine of from 20 to 24 brake horsepower, fulfilling the conditions of the Balzer contract, including the condition of fitting the present frame. You will ascertain where and how in Europe it can be obtained, getting specific information as to solvency and reputation of contractors, as to time and price, and such entirely definite statements as will be necessary for me to act on in making such a contract.

My judgment is that you can best do all this in Paris, and that it will be better for you to leave here before the close of the week, being there on the 13th at the latest. I enclose a letter of introduction for me from Mr. Maxim to the Comte de Dion, which please return.

Please give me a minutely exact statement with a drawing if possible from which one of the Comte de Dion's cylinders can be built in Washington or in New York. Please see if I can get one of them in Paris and at what cost. Perhaps I should say that when I ask you to act as though the Balzer engine was entirely abandoned, I mean that the chief object of your visit is to get something that can be absolutely relied on in its place, and it is hardly necessary to say that if you see incidentally any ways of amending it, I should like to know them, but I repeat here that the course of experiments on the engine in New York will need to absolutely come to an end with what is now being done there.

Knowing you to be so fully possessed of my wishes from our conversation, I will add nothing more.

19 July 1900—Manly in Paris to Langley in London (in part)

I shall be here for several days after you arrive, so will not trouble you now with a written digest of the motor situation, as I have not yet had an opportunity to visit the factories which are out of the city.

Nearly all of the gasoline engines used by the twenty or thirty different automobile companies are made after the general plan of the De Dion-Bouton engine, the only change being in some slight details of construction, and I think it will therefore be best to wait until you arrive, before attempting to make arrangements for the construction of a light engine, as you can then use your letter of introduction to Count De Dion and probably get the matter arranged more quickly.

30 July 1900—Langley memorandum

After two or three mischances, I obtained an interview this morning with Comte de Dion, 46 Avenue de la Grand Armee, introducing myself with letters from the Embassy and from Maxim. I took Mr. Manly with me.

De Dion is an intelligent man conversant with each detail of the subject and apparently a real inventor. He speaks excellent English.

He condemns the system of having the cylinders revolve, he having tried it himself several years ago and given it up.

The principal trouble comes from the centrifugal force piling up the oil at the end where it burns and fouls the gases. He would certainly recommend placing the cylinders side by side. He states specifically that his cylinder 10 cm. in diameter and with 11 cm. stroke develops continuously 7 brake horsepower at 2,000 revolutions. I do not understand clearly whether it would do this without limit unless there were special precautions against overheating.

This type, but using more than one cylinder so as to form a balanced machine, he thinks recommendable, and if something is to be done at once, to produce a 20 horsepower engine, he would recommend four cylinders of the same type side by side. If four such cylinders are to be used he would recommend that they be arranged to explode in the order 1–2–3–4, 1–2–3–4.

He believes, however, that there is a limiting possible weight for efficient work in this way, and that this 20 brake horse engine would involve at least 110 kilos of weight without cooling water or flywheel, both of which he thinks indispensable. He has a patent for cooling the water by tubes and radiators at one end of the cylinder where the water and steam are under a pressure which is self regulated by the rate of radiation and cooling. This pressure is something like 5 kilos to the centimeter. His system then, keeps the cylinder cool by using the same water over and over and employing consequently very little.

He has employed an alloy of aluminum largely, and strongly favors the use of it in all cases where such a metal is applicable.

He thinks of making an engine for a flying machine himself next year.

He is constantly experimenting and hopes in three or four months to have something very much lighter and more efficient than he has yet got, but would not care to give any drawings for work that is incessantly being modified.

He has no engine to sell.

He said that in this, which is the substance of his talk, he had given, he believed, the gist of what he could in the way of advice. His own successes have been obtained at the cost of incessant experiment in detail and of numberless failures, and as for my work, like any other inventor's work, he believes there is nothing for it but time and patience.

30 July 1900—Langley in Paris to Manly in Paris (in part)

In view of the advice of Mr. Maxim against a rotary engine and the strongly confirmatory opinion of the Comte de Dion in our interview this morning, of which I enclose you a memorandum, in view also of the fact that you have been unable to find anything better than the De Dion machine in London, Paris or Berlin, and in view also of your proximate return to New York and Washington, I decide as follows:

First, that further work on the original Balzer engine is to be discontinued when the experiments in actual construction are finished, which should be within a week or ten days.

Second, that Balzer should be paid for the contract price of the engine, $1,500, and the engine be taken to Washington and submitted to a brake test under the actual conditions, and again when stationary and driving the shaft with the aid of a flywheel improvised from the propellers by placing a rim on them.

I anticipate that this will cause a prejudicial shake, but if it be ineffective, some other arrangement for a flywheel can be derived.

I do not wish to make the preceding instructions absolutely mandatory, for in case that some very strong reason presents itself to you for modifying them, I will not attempt to make them absolute when I cannot tell from this side of the ocean what change may present itself.

You will, of course, do nothing without consulting Mr. Rathbun.

21 August 1900—Manly in Washington, D. C., to Langley in Europe (in part)

I landed in New York safely on Monday morning August 13th, the boat having reached the harbor too late Sunday night to move into its dock. I found the "Cymric" most pleasant there being practically no rolling or pitching perceptible, and the staterooms were very commodious and comfortable, while the table was as good or even better than that of the "Germanic". In fact, I was so very much pleased with the "Cymric" that I would without question choose it for any trip where the difference of a day or two in the length of a voyage is not important.

Immediately upon reaching New York, I went to my hotel and from there to Balzer's shop to investigate the progress that had been made during my absence. The two men, MacDonald and Newham, from the O. and F. roll, who had been working there since the day we left, had been employed the whole time in making the new and larger supply pipes and changing the combustion chambers so that these larger pipes could be connected thereto. As soon as I saw the engine, which required

80

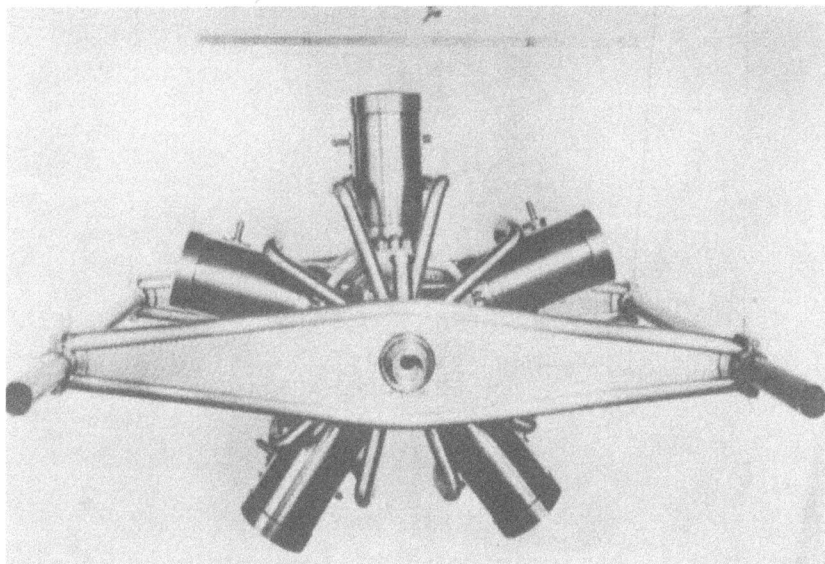

Figure 20.—Balzer-Manly engine. First stage, 8 hp, exhaust side, August 1900. (Smithsonian photo A49438.)

only a short while for adjustment before making a test, I felt certain that the changes which had been made would amount to practically nothing in increasing the power, and I accordingly told Balzer to get the engine ready for its last and final trial on Tuesday morning.

On Tuesday morning, everything being in readiness, I made a test of the engine with the result that only about six horsepower was obtained, owing to the cylinders not working properly, but as I was satisfied that any further time spent in adjustment would be utterly wasted, I directed Balzer to box the engine and all its accessories, the tools used in its construction, the framework for supporting it, and in fact, everything connected with it and ship the entire affair to Washington immediately.

I am now making preparations to test the large engine with the cylinders stationary and with a temporary arrangement for a water-jacket for keeping the cylinders cool, the cylinders of course being mounted in the circle as they have always been, and the only change being that the drum which supports them will be held stationary and the crankshaft allowed to revolve with a temporary flywheel on it. Upon the result of this test will depend my next step, for if the power and speed be obtained in this preliminary test, I will then construct permanent water-

81

FIGURE 21.—Balzer-Manly engine; First stage, 8 hp, view showing valves and ignition system, August 1900. (Smithsonian photo A49438-A.)

jackets either using the De Dion principle or a specially light condenser, and if it does not prove successful, the next step I will take will doubtless be to dismount the cylinders from the circular arrangement and mount them side by side, this last arrangement requiring five cranks on one shaft, and of course necessitating an increased weight on the shaft. The only difficulty which I anticipate in this first test which I expect to make will be with reference to the oiling of the uppermost cylinders, but I am having made a temporary arrangement for this. I now have all of the workmen engaged on the construction of the special clamps necessary for holding the drum which supports the cylinders and firmly attaching it to the bedplate upon which the cylinders will be stationary and the crank will revolve. This construction will probably require the remainder of this week and I think it possible that I may obtain this first test with the cylinders stationary by the beginning of next week, and will in any event communicate with you by next Wednesday's steamer.

No further attempts were made to develop the engine as a rotary. Under Manly it became a static watercooled radial—a more complicated, heavier, and bulkier engine—but it immediately met the horse-

power requirements. Stage one, therefore, terminated with Balzer's loss of design control over the engine on 21 August 1900. During that year, the horsepower output had dropped from 8 to 6, indicating that Balzer had retrogressed in spite of valiant efforts to improve the engine.

Chapter 4

Balzer-Manly Aero Engine, Second Stage

The most dramatic increase in power occurred during the second stage (between 21 August to 11 September 1900), when output rose from 6 to 16 horsepower. Manly had merely changed the engine from a rotary radial to a static radial by fastening the crankcase to a fixed object and allowing the crankshaft to rotate. Since the cylinders no longer rotated, they had to be cooled, temporarily with damp rags. This encouraging horsepower increase not only indicated to Manly in what direction to further develop the engine, but also assured him that the Balzer engine could be retained as the basic structure. Stage two, therefore, set the course of the engine's future development.

3 September 1900—Langley in Carlsbad, Austria, to Manly in Washington, D.C.

I have your letter of the twenty-first and while glad to hear of your safe return, I need hardly say it is with regret that I receive its bad news with regard to the Balzer engine.

I am too far from being an expert in such matters to insist on a line of conduct against your counsel, but I have an impression that unless your early efforts in remodeling the Balzer engine meet with success, it will be better not to continue them, but to let the whole thing go and to extract from it the teaching of this dearly bought experience that it is better in such things to keep in the common road where the experience of such as have found practical success seems to show that efficiency is connected with not only a very much higher speed than ever was expected from the Balzer engine, but with a form of side by side cylinders with a well worked out sparking device, from which a departure in the smallest details opens unknown chances of difficulty.

84

This at least I understand to be the gist of the counsel of both Maxim and De Dion.

In case you can certainly build a small engine of the De Dion type for the model at Washington, for something like the equivalent of the sum of seven hundred dollars which you tell me has disappeared in Balzer's hands, I think it had better be done there and that this work should go on independently of the other whatever may be done with the large one.

If you are not entirely confident of your ability to do it successfully without any new experiment, on the De Dion type so efficiently as to be an essay and model for the large one, I should like to seriously consider the building of it on this side in hands actually experienced in the work.

I shall be in England probably a month from now and I may possibly be able to arrange with Maxim for the use of a skilled workman or workmen to undertake this task of the small De Dion engine and get out the results which Maxim says have actually been obtained in an engine made under his eye, and which I detailed to you. I have not these details by me now, but I think they represented in the particular one of Maxim's construction, something like $2\frac{1}{2}$ brake horse for a cylinder 3 inches in diameter.

If you are confident of your ability to do it directly (I mean without indefinite experiment) please commence the small engine in Washington (if you have not already done so) at once. If you have any doubts on this point, then in your next letter please write me whether in your judgment it is possible or desirable to do anything in England about it (the small engine).

In case you favor this course, write me fully with plans on the ordinary De Dion type, adapted to the frame and conditions of mounting of the small engine, for I might possibly have the time to arrange to start it in London before I return, though I by no means like to do this. I should like to have you let me have your opinion as to the possibility of building the large engine even here.

I consent if you recommend, to build this small engine at Washington. I do not absolutely refuse to consider the idea of building the large one there, but if there is one thing which I am more reluctant than another to contemplate, it is the prospect of entering on a course of experiment in engine building in our shops, and I should be glad to hear where else you think it can be done and by whom.

85

8 September 1900—Manly in Washington, D.C., to Balzer in New York City

Please, *as soon as possible,* send me by mail in the enclosed "Frank," the pattern of the five pointed hub from which the brass crank shaft bearings of the engine are made.

I am having some changes made in the engine, and everything is progressing very nicely and as soon as I obtain the results I expect I will let you know the full details.

I am also expecting to make some experiments with a slightly different form of carbureter and if there is any of that Tupelo wood left I would like for you to send it to me by Express. Please, however, send the hub pattern tomorrow if possible, as I want to use it immediately.

I trust that the wagon engine is now in good working order and hope to see you sometime soon and talk over the affairs of the company.[35]

11 September 1900—Manly in Washington, D.C., to Langley in Europe

I have only time for this short note to let you know that I am exceedingly glad to be able to state that the results which I am now obtaining from the engine are of a very encouraging nature.

I made the first preliminary run on Friday, September 7th, and although the engine was not working as well as I was certain it would do later, I obtained 750 revolutions per minute with the horsepower varying between twelve and sixteen. I made another test on Saturday, having changed the conditions with the expectation of obtaining more speed, and although I was unable to get a brake test reading, due to one of the bearings overheating early in the test, yet I was much gratified at obtaining a speed of 800 revolutions with the assurance from the run that the speed could be brought still higher.[36]

Both of these tests were made using the temporary water-jacket arrangement with the cylinders stationary.[37] I am at the moment of writing this, just completing adjustments for another test this afternoon, but as it will be too late when I complete the test to get the letter off on tomorrow's steamer, I am sending this personal note to relieve, as much as possible, any anxiety you may feel in reference to the work.

---

[35] Manly is referring to an automobile company that Balzer was attempting to form.

[36] On 3 January 1900 Balzer ran the engine at 800 rpm. With the cylinders made stationary, the engine's automatic valves, freed from centrifugal and inertial forces, operated properly for the first time, hence the increased power.

[37] The "temporary water-jacket arrangement" was the use of damp cloths wrapped around the cylinders such as Balzer had used on 23 August 1899 when demonstrating the running of a single fixed cylinder to Manly.

As soon as I can get a good and entirely satisfactory test both of the highest speed obtainable and the maximum power at some certain speed, I will write you officially. If the results of the present tests justify me in believing that with the cylinders stationary and properly water-jacketed, as much as eighteen or twenty horse power may be obtained, I will immediately start the men at work on the permanent water-jackets. These water-jackets and their accessories will probably require between three weeks and a month for their completion, and I, therefore, wish to be very certain of sufficient power being obtained from this one engine before I start this construction.

12 September 1900—Telegram from Manly in Washington, D. C., to Balzer in New York City

Please send by express, immediately, tools and mandril for making large inlet pipe elbows and washers for bending tubes.

Circa 15 September 1900—Rathbun in Washington, D. C., to De Dion-Bouton Motorette Co. in New York City

I am returning to you by express this afternoon, the spark coil which was received from you a few days ago, and which upon examination has been found to be out of order. From the weakness of the spark which it gives when properly connected, it would seem that the circuit at some point in the secondary is partially broken, and as it is urgently needed in the work here, I beg to request that you will either repair it or send another in its place immediately.

18 September 1900—Manly in Washington, D. C., to Langley in Europe

Your letter from Carlsbad, of September third, acknowledging the receipt of mine of August 21st, was received last Thursday. The several questions which you have asked regarding the engines have been dwelt upon in the letters which I have written you since August 21st, but which, of course, you had not received at that time.

However, to make certain that you thoroughly understand just what I am doing with the engines, I will say that in the first place I have entirely abandoned Balzer's idea of the rotary cylinders, and that all the work which has been done on the large engine since my return and the arrival of the engine in Washington, has been with the cylinders held stationary and cooled by temporary water-jackets, and in the second place, that with the arrangement just described the results which I have obtained have encouraged me to hope that it will be possible to so modify the present engine as to obtain from it as much as 18 or 20 horse power for a weight not exceeding 200 pounds, including water-jackets, cooling water, condenser, flywheel and all other appurtenances.[38]

In my letter of last Tuesday, September 11, I stated that I was then just about to make another test on the [large] engine. The engine was started up on Tuesday afternoon but too late to get a test. However, a run was made on Wednesday, September 12, the result being that at a speed of 800 revolutions, the power varied from 12 to 16 horsepower, or about the same as the previous test. The reason of the variation in the power is due to the manner of making the brake test, the fly-wheel used being so small that as soon as the prony brake begins to heat from the absorption of the work it binds irregularly, and requires a great deal of care in properly regulating it.

I have made no more runs on the large engine since last Wednesday, as I have found it necessary to construct an arrangement to prevent the exhaust from going down on the bedplate as it does at present. This construction is now about complete, and I expect to make another run either tomorrow or the day following.

With reference to your questions regarding the advisability of seeing what can be done in England, in the way of securing the construction of the large engine and possibly the small, I will say very frankly that if you can find anyone willing to undertake the work, I would recommend that contracts be immediately entered into for the engine but at the same time, I will be very surprised if any very great assistance out of the difficulty is found in this way. At the same time, it can certainly do no harm to enter into contracts, and of course there may be a possibility of good being thus accomplished.

28 September 1900—Manly in Washington, D. C., to Balzer in New York City

I had hoped to have a chance ere this to see you and talk over the affairs of the motor company, but I have been so very busy both with the previous work and the additional caused by the two engines, that this has been impossible.

I have heard nothing from you regarding the outcome of the wagon, but I feel very certain that my fears regarding it have been entirely justified. Since bringing the two engines to Washington, I have made a most thorough and careful examination of them, and to be entirely frank with you, as I have always been, I must say that I am now *thor-*

---

[38] By converting Balzer's rotary engine to a radial Manly was able to double its horsepower—from 8 to 16—thus exceeding the contract requirements. This answers one of the problems posed in the Introduction. Later it will be seen, however, that Manly made this change for the wrong reason.

oughly and *absolutely* convinced that the rotary cylinder will never prove a success no matter how much money or time may be expended on it. The main reason why it will never be a success has escaped you and I must confess that up to the time I returned from Europe, it had escaped me, and my reasons for not having written you earlier was that I wished to be absolutely certain that I was right before calling your attention to it.

In the familiar type of stationary cylinder gasoline engine, the explosion which occurs when the piston is at the beginning of its stroke produces a pressure on the crankshaft the tangential effect of which is very small until the crank has moved through a few degrees, the pressure on the piston tends to send the crank on around in its circle, and, of course, the further the crank has moved until it reaches the mid stroke, the greater this tangential force becomes. In other words, the piston is at all times moving in the exact direction in which the force of the explosion tends to send it. Now in the rotary cylinder this is not the case, for in this case the explosion which occurs between the head of the cylinder and the piston would tend to send the cylinder directly out, and this, of course, produces an enormous strain on the bedplate and from the very fact of the rotary motion of the cylinder at *no* time is the cylinder moving in the direction in which the explosion tends to send it, and even at mid stroke the tangential force is almost nothing. Now in the stationary cylinder engine at mid stroke the crank is perpendicular and the tangential force on the crankshaft (neglecting the angularity of the connecting rod) is equal to the full pressure on the piston, whereas in the rotary cylinder at no time is the tangential force on the cylinder equal to the pressure on the piston, and in fact it is *never even equal to one half this pressure.* In other words, in the rotary cylinder the explosion is at all times tending to send the cylinder directly away from the center of the shaft, whereas the rotary drum compels it to move in a circle, and it was this very thing which has made it impossible to speed the large engine above 375 revolutions as a maximum.[39]

---

[39] Manly had devised an erroneous theory to explain the operation of the rotary engine, the conclusion of which was that the rotary only developed one half as much power as a radial of the same size. When he actually got twice as much power (16 h.p.) from the engine as Balzer had (8 h.p.), Manly considered his theory proven; yet basically all he had done was convert the engine from a rotary to a radial. The theory of operation of a static radial or rotary engine is identical for both types of engine. The added efficiency was due to a function of the valves. It should also be noted that Balzer had the engine running at 800 rpm on 3 January 1900 (see page 57).

Wishing to be absolutely certain about this point before bringing the matter to your attention, I have made some very radical changes in the large engine, and am now making some still further changes. The first changes were made immediately upon arrival of the engines in Washington, and before the close of the second week after their arrival here (that is before the last of August), I had obtained more than double the power which the engine had ever previously developed, and had experienced absolutely no difficulty in obtaining more than 800 revolutions per minute.

I need hardly say that there is no one who is more anxious to see you succeed or is more willing to be of any assistance possible, and it is this very reason which causes me to say to you very frankly now, that before the wagon can be a success, either from an engineering or commercial point of view, it is absolutely necessary that the rotary cylinder be abandoned.

If you see any reasons that cause you to think my above conclusions regarding the engine are at fault, do not hesitate to write fully and freely to me about it, because I am fully aware of the difficulty that one always meets in giving up a thing on which one has spent six of the best years of his life.[40]

I must close now but hope you will write me fully and freely about the affairs of the company, and I trust will hear from you by Sunday night or Monday morning.

29 September 1900—Langley in Paris to Rathbun in Washington, D. C. (in part)

It is clearly impossible to carry on a written correspondence any longer at the eleventh hour. I have already cabled you to get a clear written statement which may decide me.

I now add that, on receipt of this, if such a clear statement has not been already given that Mr. Manly should through you, cable me something more positive than is contained in his letter just received [September 18]. In other words, it is just that the responsibility of the decision should rest on him, and that he express it one way or the other, either saying that he will build something in Washington which will do the work, or that I had better abandon hope of his doing so, and attempt to buy on this side with all the difficulties in the way. There is no middle course, and he as an engineer, and on the ground, must take

[40] On 14 October 1900 Balzer wrote to Manly disagreeing with his rotary engine theory; and on the 18th Manly wrote back to him reaffirming his faith in the erroneous theory.

the responsibility of advising, and say in substance, "I can build here in reasonable time" or, "I give it up". I have got nothing yet of the builders here.

If Mr. Manly has not already written positively let him cable a few words which I shall get before it is too late to make some arrangement here.

9 October 1900—Cable from Manly in Washington, D. C., to Langley in London

Manly can build here in reasonable time.

27 October 1900—Wells diary

Mr. Manly orders some platinum wire today from Lambie to replace that in the sparking plugs for the large engine.[41]

30 October 1900—Manly waste book entry (in part)

The change in the sparking plugs being completed, they were put in place and a preliminary run with a tachometer was made to see if the change in the sparking plugs would overcome the trouble from the lubrication short-circuiting the plug. The engine started up without any difficulty, only one or two turns being necessary, and was allowed to run for two or three minutes.

It was found that the sparking was perfect, the engine never since it was built having run so smoothly.[42]

31 October 1900—Manly waste book entry

I this morning had the two lower cylinders taken off and cleaned out with gasoline, and it was found there was quite a bit of burned graphite and oil in both of these cylinders. All the piston oil cups were then filled with oil, the two lower cylinders replaced, and the water jackets

---

[41] *Langley Memoir on Mechanical Flight* (pages 221 and 222) ; Considerable difficulty was at first experienced with the spark plugs from a coating ot soot (resulting from the incomplete combustion of the gas and oil in the cylinder at the time of explosion) which formed on the porcelain and thereby caused a short-circuit, preventing the plug from working properly. This was overcome by extending the metal portion of the plug for some distance into the cylinder, and for something like three-quarters of an inch beyond the end of the porcelain insulator. The terminal which passed through the insulator was also extended for something like half an inch beyond the porcelain and bent to a proper extent to co-act with a piece of platinum wire inserted in the interior wall of the plug which formed the other terminal. After making this improvement in the plugs practically no difficulty was experienced from short-circuits caused by soot.

[42] This change undoubtedly refers to the spark plugs. See footnote 41.

put on ready for a trial, the carbureter having had about a gallon of gasoline put in it. About 10 o'clock an attempt was made to start the engine, and upon its failing to start, and after making sure that everything else was correct, the carbureter was examined and found to be filled with gasoline. The superfluous gasoline was emptied back into the can, and upon again starting the engine, everything was found to work perfectly. After a short run of only about two minutes premature explosion set in due to the present temporary water jackets being so soaked with oil that they did not hold water.

The engine was accordingly shut down, and some fresh cloth was gotten and new jackets made from it. At two o'clock, the new jackets being completed and adjusted to the cylinders, a run was made in which the maximum recorded revolutions was about 650 with only four of the cylinders working. The run lasted several minutes, but it was useless to prolong it until all the cylinders were working, and the engine was accordingly shut down and it was found that one of the sparking plugs was not working properly. This plug was repaired and the engine was immediately gotten ready for another trial.

Three more runs were made with practically the same result, there being first trouble with one cylinder and then with another, due to either water or surplus oil having gotten down into the cylinder and interfered with the sparking, to the secondary wires working loose from the plugs, etc.

I am having McDonald remove the springs from the main valves and will have him wind some new springs the first thing in the morning from some stiffer wire, the present springs I have being too weak at the start, and having become weaker due to the excessive heating of the cylinders. I shall also have the valve stems of these main valves bored out so as to lighten up the valves, thus insuring quicker and more certain closing of the valves.

2 November 1900—Manly waste book entry (in part)

The drilling out of the valve actuating rods and the valves was completed about 11 o'clock this morning and the valves with their springs, etc., were put back into place and preparations made for a run this afternoon, the joints being adjusted to the cylinders. The valve actuating rods with the rollers formerly weighed 87 grammes and the main valve weighed 52 grammes. The valves now weigh 43 grammes, and the actuating rods 61 grammes. This is inclusive of the springs and nuts.

The connection was repaired, the water jackets wetted down, and another run with practically the same results was obtained, the Secretary witnessing both runs.

Immediately after luncheon I made another run with the Prony brake in place and the propeller off, to see whether the present sparking arrangement will allow the engine to speed up to its former free rate of 850 rpm. After two short runs it was found that the engine even running free does not speed over 700 rpm, and I will therefore investigate the cause of this later.

4 November 1900—Manly waste book entry

I have this morning broached the subject to the Secretary of the construction of a new and more powerful engine for the large Aerodrome. He, however, seems very much opposed to it on the ground that the present engine had been delayed almost two years while it was in the hands of Balzer, and that all during that time it was a source of aggravation and almost despair, and that it was only after I personally took the responsibility of producing a suitable engine, and made such a complete change in the present one to bring success out of failure, and that he is therefore willing to "let well enough alone", and to depend on using the present engine.[43] However, I am still strongly in favor of the construction of a new and more powerful engine, and shall not be content until work on it actually commences.

7 November 1900—Manly waste book entry (in part)

McDonald will make some new caps for the pistons of the large engine. These new caps for the pistons of the large engine are to determine what effect raising the compression will have on the work of the engine as I shall want to raise the compression slightly when I make the new and lighter pistons for the engine. At present the compression space in the large engine is about 40 per cent of the volume swept through by the piston. These new caps on the pistons will reduce the compression space to about 25 per cent of the volume swept through by the piston which should raise the mean effective pressure to between 75 and 80 lbs. which also means a slight increase of power; but it may also increase the vibration of the engine, and in case this is so, it will probably be best not to raise the compression so much. However, it is impossible to say just what the effect will be until I make a trial with the increased compression.

---

[43] The "complete change" consisted of changing the engine from a rotary to a radial. This was done after a consultation with Balzer who indicated that it would be practical.

14 November 1900—Manly waste book entry (in part)

I will then put him [Newham] to work in the lower room, South Shed getting out some disks 1/8 in. thick which will be placed on the ends of the pistons of the large engine, to see what effect the increased compression will have on its running.

14 November 1900—Manly waste book entry (in part)

Russell has now about completed the stuffing boxes for the water jackets, and should be ready to fit these to the cylinders and jackets by tomorrow. Before any further work is done on the jackets, however, I shall have Russell cut the bay window jackets from the piston chambers of the cylinders and insert circular pieces in their places so as to have the water jackets encircle the cylinders and the combustion chamber at a uniform distance. These bay window projections were put on in New York on the first of last June to enable the wiping spark to properly work, but are now not necessary, and merely serve as a receptacle for burnt gasses.[44]

If the sparking plugs in the heads of the cylinders of the small engine demonstrate that there is no trouble from their becoming fouled more rapidly than when they are in the combustion chamber, I shall probably change the sparking plugs in the large cylinders to the heads, change the inlet valves in the caps of the combustion chambers, and entirely do away with the valve chambers on these cylinders. The object of this change would be twofold; first in order to get rid of the valve chambers, and second in order to get the sparking plug where the combustion would be more nearly instantaneous than when it has to travel through the present inadequate ports in order to ignite the main charge in the cylinder proper. The main valve would then become the exhaust valve, and the present exhaust valve would be entirely done away with.[45]

26 February 1901—Wells diary (in part)

A preliminary run obtaining 700 rpm was made on the large engine late this afternoon. Other runs will be made in the morning.

1 March 1901—Wells diary (in part)

The Secretary goes to Lower Room, South Shed this afternoon about

---

[44] Manly is referring to necessary changes since the ignition system of the engine was modified from low to high tension.

[45] An excellent idea—This change simplified the engine, reduced its weight, and permitted it to breathe more freely.

3:30, but does not wait to see test of large engine which when started at 4 o'clock by Mr. Manly runs 3 minutes at approx. 800 rpm which indicates 24 hp. This was with propeller attached.

2 March 1901—Wells diary

A Prony brake test of the large engine running at 600 rpm was made this afternoon, which showed the engine developed 18 hp at this speed.

5 March 1901—Langley to Captain Lewis both in Washington, D. C.

Referring to my letter of February 23rd, I would say that if you care to see a brake test, I could have one for you any forenoon this week which you may indicate.

I am in hopes to show you 18 horsepower at the brake for an engine which with cooling water and all complete, weighs less than 200 pounds. It has actually done this, and if it is not fractious, will do it in your sight I hope, though I have not yet got it to run with absolute uniformity.

12 March 1901—Wells diary entry by Manly (in part)

Made 4 runs on large engine, each of which was of short duration due to the breaking of the water connections, but the engine working favorably and showing slightly over 40 lbs. on the brake at 700 rpm with each cylinder working intermittently.

Started 5th run in the afternoon and found cylinder #1 full of water. The engine was dismantled and cylinder taken off, and upon putting hydraulic pressure upon the water jackets, it was found that the asbestos packing under the cap was broken and had sprung a leak. New packing put in and assembling the engine preparatory to trial first thing in the morning left in charge of McDonald.

Unless some unforseen difficulty arises the engine should be in proper working order so that Captain Lewis can see it when he comes down tomorrow.

13 March 1901—Wells diary (in part)

Captain I. N. Lewis, Recorder of the Board of Ordnance and Fortification, War Department, came down at the Secretary's request this afternoon at 1:30 to see a brake trial of the large engine, and look at the work in progress.

He saw both the large and small engines running. The large one did not work well owing to the non-working of a cylinder, but gave a pull on the scale of from 25 to 30 lbs.

The small engine worked exceedingly well after a short trouble in the beginning.

The maximum output of 18 horsepower was developed in the stage two configuration on 2 March 1901. This was more than twice the power that Balzer had been able to obtain in over one and a half years. The only major design change over stage one was the addition of the water jackets. Therefore, although Balzer's engine had had the potential to meet the contract requirement for 12 horsepower, it was Manly who earned the credit for doing so.

Chapter 5

Balzer-Manly Aero Engine, Third Stage

*O*n 28 June 1901, the engine developed 25 horsepower and maintained this level during 1902. The major design change in stage three was discarding Balzer's heavy "ball and socket" pistons for the modern light-weight "piston pin" type, which is universally used to this day.

15 March 1901—Langley waste book entry

On the 13th Captain Lewis, Recorder of the Board, came by my invitation to see a brake test of the actual engine. It was a failure.

In answer to my subsequent questions I obtained from Mr. Manly the following memorandum.

Mr. Manly says in relation to the trial of yesterday that the present engine, which has yielded 21½ hp at the brake, is but a patched up thing, and cannot be counted on. Independently of this the 5 cylinder engine can never in theory be a perfectly balanced one; and the weight of the present pistons considered, it is certain that even if it ran, the vibration would be too great for the actual frame.[46]

Mr. Manly would like to do three things, two of them immediate and practical:

1. To put into the present patched engine as it exists, light pistons with the present patched up water jackets, these pistons to weigh perhaps 4 lbs. instead of the present 6½ lbs. This first change (which is now under way) is purely experimental, and will be completed in a week or ten days.

2. If the vibration cannot be cured by lightening these pistons, it

---

[46] The 5-cylinder configuration in radial form is a perfectly valid one from the standpoint of balance, and the heavy pistons were not a liability when the engine was run as a rotary as there was no absolute reciprocation.

will next be in order to make entirely new castings for pistons which will give decreased compression in the present cylinders, these new pistons being also of the lighter weight; and an attempt made to obtain sufficient power by making up in the speed of the engine what was lost in the explosive pressure. The engine in its final form is held up until these experiments with the pistons are complete, though the work is going on on the cylinders for them.

This second stage of experiment can only be met, with the engine designed to be completed in June, on the engine itself; that is, with the new cylinders, and if this fails to control the vibration, we are at the end of any possibility we can now see of using the 5 cylinder engine.

3. If the 5 cylinder engine does not work satisfactorily, Mr. Manly can suggest nothing but the building of the 6 cylinder one, which will almost necessarily run without prejudicial vibration, but which it may be practically impossible to undertake with our time and means.

In Manly's belief the chances of success with the 5 cylinder engine are good enough to warrant the continuance of the work on it, leaving the other questions open.

16 March 1901—Memorandum by Langley and Manly

I wrote and telephoned to Captain Lewis that he could see a brake trial of the engine this afternoon, if he could come down at a little after one o'clock. He replied that he could not get here until 3:30. I said that the trial would be ready for him to see at that hour, but that I had an engagement which would prevent my being present. He came, and Mr. Manly reports as follows:

"Captain Lewis arrived promptly at 3:30, and was met in the reception room by Mr. Manly, and went immediately to the Lower Room of the South Shed, where the trials are being held.

The [large] engine was started up immediately, and a continuous run of about 12 or 15 minutes was made. The brake varied slightly, being a trifle higher than the reading recorded below at the beginning, but falling off toward the middle of the run owing to the imperfect lubrication of the cylinders when the lubricating oil commenced to be carbonized by the excessive heating, the circulation in the water jackets being imperfect during this run. The least or commercial reading of the brake was 35 lbs. at 750 rpm on a Prony brake arm of four feet, and this result was maintained during the entire run, and as stated above, was slightly more at the beginning and represents a minimum of somewhat over 17 horsepower.

The imperfection in the circulation of the cooling water being remedied, a second run was started, but it was found that excessive heat had melted two of the sparking plugs. However, others were immediately substituted and the engine again started up without any difficulty. The results of this second run were practically the same as those of the first, and it should be noted that in the second run, all of the lubricating oil in the piston oil cups had been used up and the lubrication of the cylinders was therefore not so perfect as in the first trial. In this second run the water inlet pipe on cylinder #2 developed a fracture and began to seriously leak.

The break in the water connection of cylinder #2 was temporarily repaired by some cloths, and a third and short run made to demonstrate the extent of the reliability of the engine. The engine was started up immediately without any difficulty, only one or two turns being made by hand in order to take in gas from the carbureter. The result of this third run was practically the same as that of the first and second, and the engine was several times speeded up during the run in order to demonstrate the very high speed at which it was possible to work it.

It is particularly to be noted that at all these trials the cylinders were dirty from lack of the considerable time needed to dismount them to clean them, but that when clean and fresh they have been known to give a great deal more, the highest ever having been obtained being 24 horse and 21 on several other occasions.

The result of these trials was that the engine had actually given a minimum of 17 horse under the imperfect conditions in which it was tried.

Captain Lewis expressed himself as greatly pleased with the results, which he considered to show much the most considerable advance in engine building that has ever been made.

22 March 1901—F. W. Hadley in Washington, D. C., to the De Dion-Bouton Motorette Co., 37th & Church Lane, Brooklyn, New York

I am authorized by the Secretary to inquire if you can furnish the Institution with a small quantity of the cement which you use in cementing into place the long platinum wire in the sparking plugs.

The cement is wanted in some special research work now in progress at the Institution, and if you can furnish it, please send about a table-spoonful, together with your bill, under the enclosed frank.

29 April 1901—Wells diary

Mr. Manly is reassembling the present large engine, putting in the new light pistons which have been made for it and for the new engine, and expects to run it after these pistons have been "worn" in the old cylinders for 2 or 3 days.

1 May 1901—Manley in Washington, D. C., to Balzer in New York

From your telegram of the 26th instant, I judge that you are back at work at the shop, though I have not yet received the letter which you said in your telegram you would write me.

I find that the crankshaft in the large engine has gotten slightly bent owing to the excessive power which I have been obtaining from it. When you first started to build the engine you turned up one crankshaft for it and had it about half complete when you noticed a small flaw in the wrist pin, and the crank was therefore discarded and a new one made. When I was at the shop last spring I noticed this old unfinished crankshaft lying near the carpenter bench in the upper room, and my recollection is that the flaw in the wrist pin was a very small one indeed.

If you have not destroyed this crankshaft and can get it out of the shop for me, I wish you would send it to me (addressing it: Smithsonian Institution, O. and F. acct.) by express as soon as possible and I will see that you are paid what is proper for it.

Let me hear from you regarding the affairs of the Company, as you well know I am very deeply interested in them.

2 May 1901—Wells diary

The large engine with the new pistons has been running all of today under the power of an electric motor, and it will probably soon be in fit condition to run under its own power.

28 June 1901—Wells diary (in part)

Mr. Manly made several runs on the large engine with the new pistons, and with it drove the 2 meter propeller at a speed varying from 850 to 875 rpm. The average power developed in the various runs was between 25 and 30 horsepower, which compared with the power developed on March 16, when Capt. Lewis witnessed the test, shows for a speed of 850 rpm 8½ hp more than at that time shown on the brake, the brake showing very much less power than the calculations based on the work of the propeller, which at that time was 22½ hp and which would make the present test show a horsepower of over 30, or to be more exact 33¾. This increase in power is entirely due to the latest changes in the pistons which Mr. Manly has made.

1 January 1901—Manly to Langley both in Washington, D.C. (in part)

When I assumed the responsibility of producing an engine suitable for the aerodrome, I fully expected that it would be necessary to construct an entirely new and larger engine, for I deemed it unsafe to launch the aerodrome with an engine which could develop the minimum power required *only* when it was working at its very best. I have since found that by constructing a new set of cylinders of a larger diameter (including of course new pistons, piston rods and crank) it will be possible to provide an engine which will furnish when working at its very best at least 25 or 26 horsepower, which it would therefore be safe to depend on developing, under the conditions of actual flight, ample power. I never expected to utilize the present engine except for experimental purposes, so that when I did undertake a new engine there would be no experiment connected with it; and I now feel that although there are still some things which may be learned from the present cylinders, yet owing to the pressure for time, it will be better to immediately construct the new set of cylinders and thus have the final engine in a finished condition as soon as possible. It should also be remembered as stated in the earlier part of this report that I am designing the new cylinders in such a way that none of the essential parts of the engine as it exists at present (such as the circular bed-plate, sparking arrangement, valve rods, etc.) will be altered and it will thus be possible at all times, in case it is required, to use either set of cylinders and thus have always on hand a reserve engine.

I may recall in this connection the fact that the French engine builders are very much opposed to the steel cylinders having a cast iron lining, they maintaining that it is impossible to rely on such a construction, although they recognize that it is in this direction that the greatest saving in weight can be made. This same opinion on the subject would probably be confirmed by engine builders of this country, and if cylinders giving satisfactory results had not already been constructed in this way, it would be best to accept their judgment in the matter. However, it is impossible to give this work out under contract since I know of no shops outside of Mr. Balzer's which are well enough acquainted with this kind of work to do it properly, and as Mr. Balzer is at present engaged in other work, it is impossible for him to do it; so that if it is to be done, it must be done in our own shops and under the most careful supervision. Of course, if there were no other work to be done, the present equipment of machine tools would serve to rapidly complete the engine, but the present equipment will certainly be taxed to its utmost, as it has always been, in completing other essential parts of the work. It

101

will therefore be necessary in order to complete these cylinders, including their pistons, water jackets, etc. within the time when they will be required, to install at least two additional lathes, and employ at least two additional skilled machinists who are accustomed to this kind of work. Regardless of whether the present cylinders or new ones are used, it will be necessary to construct a light condenser and pump capable of taking care of the water required for cooling the cylinders. It will also be necessary to provide the carbureter and tank for the fuel, as well as new propeller and transmission shafts for the frame, as the shafts at present in place will probably not prove strong enough. Outside of minor accessories for the engine, such as providing means to allow the aeronaut to properly regulate the engine from his seat, the above is about all that can be at present anticipated with reference to the engine.[47]

14 November 1900—Manly waste book entry (in part)

Manly already knew exactly how he would construct the new cylinders as this partial quotation indicates.

While in New York last Saturday at the Automobile Show at Madison Square Garden, I noticed that Janney, Steinmetz and Company are now making cylinders from 5 in. to 16 in. in diameter of cold drawn steel which are closed at one end by circular domes, the domes and walls all being in one solid piece. Since seeing these cylinders I am thinking very strongly of taking the present large engine and making new cylinders for it by turning out a 5 in. tube to $5\frac{1}{8}$ in. internal diameter, lining it with a 1/16 in. extra iron, and brazing the combustion chamber to the side of the cylinder. By using the cylinders closed at one end the most tedious part of the construction of new cylinders would be done away with since the heads and combustion chambers as formerly made from the solid could now be superseded by the plain combustion chamber, all of the work on which would be simple lathe work. With the present supporting drum and a new crank, for a longer bearing surface for the piston rod brasses, the engine should develop not less than 25 hp., and I feel very sure it would develop as much as 28. However, I do not care to consider construction until I have made the further experiments on the present engine to determine the advantage or disadvantage of the sparking plugs being in the heads of the cylinders and the amount of space by which the water jackets should be separated from the cylinders in order to obtain just sufficient water to keep the cylinders cool, and also until I have made a brake test of the engine

---

[47] See entry of 4 November 1900 (p. 93) regarding the first time Manly broached the subject of building a "new" engine to Langley.

and determine exactly and directly how much power it is now developing.

However, if the tests on the present large engine do show that it will be advisable to construct larger cylinders, I think these new cylinders, built as above described, can be without question completed by 5 men in 4 weeks time, and a new crank, and all other necessary changes could be made by one extra man in the same length of time, so that if these points are determined by the first of January, 1901, there should certainly be no delay caused by having this work done in outside shops.

To summarize, the major phases of development during the third stage were: (1) The use of new light weight pistons permitted a higher rpm and a higher compression ratio. These pistons of the De Dion-Bouton type raised the engine's power from 16 or 17 horsepower to about 25 horsepower. (2) Another feature copied from the De Dion-Bouton engine was the modern high tension rather than low tension ignition system which allowed the engine to run more smoothly at the higher rpms. (3) A permanent cooling system was devised consisting of cylinders with full length water jackets, a circulating pump, and a radiator composed of finned tubes. This in theory permitted runs of hours instead of minutes, and was therefore a great improvement over the previous water-soaked rags. On the other hand had the original rotary design (stage one) been retained and developed as such, the weight and complications of a water cooling system would have been eliminated.

Chapter 6

Balzer-Manly Aero Engine, Fourth Stage

*B*etween 14 and 19 November 1900 Manly received permission from Langley to order new larger cylinders for the engine, thereby increasing its displacement from approximately 380 cubic inches to 540 cubic inches. This change constituted stage four and by 23 March 1903, 52 horsepower was developed.

19 November 1900—Manly to Janney, Steinmetz and Company, Drexel Building, Philadelphia, Pennsylvania

I am authorized by the Secretary to inquire at what price and how soon after receipt of order you can furnish five seamless steel tubes closed at one end, 5 inches internal diameter with a $\frac{1}{8}$ inch wall and 12 inches long.

The closed end which is drawn from the solid and joined to the tube without any seam, should have a radius of curvature of about twice the diameter of the tube.

Please also state what difference in the internal diameter at the two respective ends of the tubes should be expected and allowed for.

6 February 1901—Manly in Washington, D.C., to Balzer in New York

I have been making some further changes on the original cylinders of the large engine and want to borrow the taper mandril which you used in making them and which fitted the inside of the cylinders. I think you will understand what I mean. I am not certain whether this screwed on to the spindles of the lathe or whether it was bolted to the face plate, but in either case I think I shall have no trouble in using it here, and if you will be good enough to ship it to me by express, charges collect, as soon as possible, I will thank you very much.

I would also like to know the name and address (Pugsley, I think) of the man who was agent for the Franklin Stock Cylinder Oil, as I shall probably want to order some from him right away.

I am sorry you have been having so much trouble with the wagon now in hand, but hope that everything connected with it is now in good shape. Let me hear from you when you can find time to write.

18 February 1901—Wells diary

The piston castings for the new engine received this morning from Erie Foundry Company and sent to lower room South Shed. Patterns returned with them.

20 February 1901—Manly in Washington, D.C., to The Erie Foundry Company, Erie, Pennsylvania

The piston castings were received on February 18th, and so far as they have been examined, prove to be unusually sound.

I enclose a sketch of two patterns from which I would like to have you submit an estimate for some castings. Twelve castings of pattern No. 1 are to be made, and as these castings are to be used as linings for gas engine cylinders, and will not be more than $\frac{1}{16}$ in. thick when they are machined and shrunk in, they must be of a good close grained gray iron of medium hardness, (slightly harder than the piston castings and yet not too hard) and *entirely* free from all blow and pin holes.

Eight castings of pattern No. 2 are to be made, and as they are to be used as piston rings, they must also be of good gray iron of a little closer grain and slightly harder than the above linings, and *entirely* free from all blow and pin holes.

The castings from pattern No. 1 weigh approximately 35 lbs. each, and from No. 2 approximately 15 lbs. each, and I desire that you will let me know immediately at what price per pound you can furnish the entire lot of castings, and also the shortest time that you can make shipment after receipt of patterns.

20 August 1901—Manly in Washington, D.C., to Langley in Newport, Rhode Island

I have all of the accessories connected with the large engine now fully in hand, and am completing them as rapidly as possible, and am also getting the necessary materials on hand for making as rapid repairs as possible to the frame and power transmission parts, in case there is any breakage or mishap when the large engine is put to work in its frame.

I have been somewhat hampered for some weeks now by first one

105

man being sick and then another, due to the effects of the heat, but all of the men are back at work now, and on the whole, I feel very well satisfied with the progress of the work.

3 September 1901—Manly in Washington, D. C., to Langley in Baddeck, Nova Scotia (in part)

I beg leave to submit the following brief report on the present condition of the aerodromic work.

The work on the large engine and its accessories including the water cooling system of jackets, condenser and pump is progressing as well as might be expected, considering the very great delays which have been experienced in it, caused by having to set aside this work for several weeks this summer in order to use the few large lathes we have to rush certain repairs and changes which have been necessary in the small aerodrome and its engine. The finishing cut is now being taken in the steel shells for the large cylinders, and this cut should be completed and the cast iron liners shrunk into place by the close of the present week. As soon as the liners are shrunk in, the jackets, which have already been fitted to the cylinders are to be brazed into place and the cylinders then bored out and finished up. These latter two operations will probably require from now until the twentieth of September for their completion. By this time, however, I hope to have all necessary accessories, such as carbureter, tanks, specially designed prony brake for absorbing and measuring the power of the engine without endangering it, and the new propeller and transmission shafts with their larger gears completed so that the brake trials can be had without delay and the engine then put to work in the aerodrome frame.[48]

11 September 1901—Wells diary

Ludewig is making patterns for the large dynamometer to be used in connection with the new engine when it is completed.

12 September 1901—Wells diary

Russell is at work under Mr. Manly's directions shrinking a liner in one of the new cylinders, and brazing the water jacket on cylinder.

25 September 1901—Wells diary (in part)

The shrinking in of the remaining cast iron liners was done by McDonald under Mr. Manly's direction. The whole 5 cylinders of the

---

[48] A water absorption type of dynamometer was used for measuring power. Two more years were to pass before the engine was put to the acid test! Balzer's delay now seems more understandable.

106

new large engine are being pushed to completion now, the liners being bored out, and the water jackets being attached.

26 September 1901—Wells diary (in part)

Mr. Manly [is] brazing the water jackets on the new cylinders today.[49]

2 October 1901—Wells diary

Mr. Manly puts the water pressure on the new water jackets today and finds that two or three of them leak badly which will necessitate the making of new water jackets for these cylinders, and as some of the leaks are in the cylinder head itself, the linings will have to be taken out, and consequently new castings will have to be ordered and bored as well as new water jackets made, and three new steel shells will also be ordered from Janney, Steinmetz and Company to replace the cylinders themselves.

8 November 1901—waste book entry
January 1, 1899—October 15, 1901
Large aerodrome:

Old Engine — In assisting Balzer — 1900 — $350 —	T. $350
Old Engine – Reconstruction and experimental tests in S. I.	
Shops – 1900 – $650 – 1901 – $1,050	T. $1,700
New and larger engine (engine proper) – 1901 – $1,450	T. $1,450
Condenser – 1901 – $130	T. $ 130
Dynamometer – 1901 – $60	T. $ 60
Paid Balzer on contract – $1,500	T. $1,500
	$5,190

9 November 1901—Wells diary

Hewitt, Newham, and McDonald are all at work finishing up the new large cylinders, and Mr. Manly hopes to have this new large engine finished, assembled, and ready for shop trials in the near future.

13 November 1901—Wells diary (in part)

Mr. Karr gives the Secretary a recommendation as requested by the

---

[49] Perhaps the most difficult operation in building the engine was brazing the water jackets onto the cylinders, since the engine had been designed for aircooling rather than watercooling. As a result, large areas of metal had to be brazed. The intense heat required tended to warp the thin jackets and they invariably failed the water pressure tests. Finally, when Russell, one of the best mechanics, failed to solve the problem, Manly undertook to do the brazing himself. After enduring intense heat at close quarters for many days, thereby permanently impairing his health, Manly succeeded in accomplishing the task.

latter in regard to funds for the continuance of the aerodromic work; [50] that what is known as the Bell Fund of $5,000 and the Kidder Fund of $5,000 be both set aside (making $10,000 in all) and jointly forming a fund to be called the "Bell and Kidder Fund" and to be disbursed in connection with the aerodromic work in the regular form pursued in regard to the routine Smithsonian accounts. The Secretary approves this recommendation.

6 January 1902—Wells diary

All of the men away on leave reported for work this morning (McDonald, Hewitt, and Newham) and Mr. Manly makes another trial of the engine, but the push rods for the exhaust valves still smash up causing the abandonment of the run, and Mr. Manly decides to make certain changes in the exhaust cam mechanism.

8 January 1902—Wells diary

Mr. Manly makes another trial of the large engine today with the slant on the exhaust cam greatly reduced, and finds that the push rods which lift the exhaust valves now stand up to their work; but owing to the "wobbling" of the dynamometers due to their flimsy supports, he is unwilling to let the engine run at full speed and holds it down to about 400 rpm for a 5 or 6 minute run.

Mr. Manly decides to add further balance weight to the flywheels, and puts one machinist at work fitting this additional balance weight. The balance weights on the flywheels now merely balance the crank brasses, and 1/2 the weight of the piston rods.

9 January 1902—Wells diary

Mr. Manly makes another run on large engine today with the extra balance weights on the flywheels to counteract the effect of one piston, and finds the vibration greatly reduced; but owing to the flimsy construction of the wooden bracing which supports the dynamometers, considers it unsafe to allow the engine to run at full speed, and therefore holds it down for 5 or 6 minutes run to a speed of about 500 rpm, the dynamometers recording a pull of about 50 lbs. each.

11 January 1902—Wells diary

The extra wooden bracing for testing frame of large engine being completed, and the bearings for the dynamometer lined up with the engine, the dynamometers were coupled up to the engine shaft this morn-

---

[50] The $50,000 allotted by the Board of Ordnance and Fortification had been spent.

ing preparatory to making a run on the engine. The engine was started up at 2 o'clock, started at the first turn after the current was thrown in, and a run of 10 or 12 minutes at a speed of from 900 to 950 rpm was made. The outer drums of the dynamometers still bind in their bearings so that the spring balance readings are inaccurate, for the readings of the scale show the same pull of 50 lbs. at 500 rpm that they do at 950 rpm, whereas the scale readings at 950 rpm should be nearly 4 times what they are at 500 since the pull goes up as to the square of the speed. Engine ran perfectly without a stop, all of the cylinders working in proper order, though the run was stopped to repair the primary sparker, one of the brushes of which got out of line, and cut during the run. The primary sparker being repaired, Mr. Manly expects to make another run on Monday.

Mr. Manly was exceedingly well pleased with the results of the trial.

16 January 1902—Wells diary

First test today at 11:30 a.m.—450 rpm—pulled down 270 lbs. on scale. Too much water in dynamometer. Ran off some water in dynamometer and at 1:30 got a run of 500 rpm, scale reading 225 lbs. One of balance wheels being out of true, tests had to stop. [Horsepower developed, 25.]

Mr. Manly then sets to work having balance wheel trued up.

17 January 1902—Wells diary (in part)

Engine taken apart, and pistons being lightened up to decrease vibration, and increase speed. Reinforcing specially built balance wheels, which had weakened from high speed.

On taking engine apart, all working parts found to be in extraordinary good condition, which ranks it far above the old Balzer engine.

23-24 January 1902—Wells diary

The new nuts for the spokes of the flywheels being finished, and the wheels reassembled, Mr. Manly has engine connected up to the dynamometers for a trial in the testing frame. The engine starts up readily upon making a few turns to draw in the gas, and flywheels appear to be holding true. Engine had been developing about 25 hp at 600 rpm for about 10 minutes when there was a sudden jerk on the port dynamometer, the scales recording a pull of about 350 lbs. and the engine dropping down in speed but tending to turn at about 200 rpm, when Mr. Manly shuts off engine to ascertain what has happened. Upon investigation he finds that a piece of steel about ½ in. long by ⅜ in. diameter, which through the carelessness of the workmen had been left in the dy-

109

namometer in reassembling it, had gotten wedged between the rotary and stationary plates of the dynamometer thus causing several of the sectors of one of the rotary plates to be twisted, bent and broken, thus wedging the dynamometer.

The port dynamometer being repaired and reassembled, Mr. Manly makes another run on engine in testing frame. Engine starts up readily and has been running about 4 minutes when suddenly engine commences to smash itself all to pieces on the inside, and Mr. Manly shuts it off immediately. Upon investigation it is found that three of the five crank pin brasses which fasten the piston rods to the crank have broken, allowing the crank to smash them into the sides of the cylinders, and upon first examination three of the cylinders appear almost irreparably damaged. Engine is immediately dismantled and upon closer investigation, it is found that cylinder No. 5 has been smashed by its own piston rod, and that of No. 4 being forced into the lower inch of length, stripping and splitting the steel, and smashing the cast iron lining. Cylinder No. 4 has lower inch strip and liner bottom smashed to pieces. Cylinder No. 3 same as No. 4. Cylinder No. 1 lower inch strip in one piece, and liner has small piece broken, but will not need to be pieced. Cylinder No. 2 uninjured.

25 January 1902 —Manly to Langley both in Washington, D.C.

I have verbally reported to you the success of the new engine which has been developing 25 hp right along, and more than 30 hp at its best. I have run it as high as 950 rpm, but last night while running it at a rate of 675 rpm the wrist pin bearings which bind the wrist pins to the connecting rods apparently gave away, and four cylinders out of five were wrecked, though not beyond repair.

Where the steel has been drawn out of shape I have got to draw it back into shape, and I will give you next week an approximate estimate of the time I think it will take to put the whole thing in order again.

Following your instructions, I have ordered four more steel shells. These cost approximately $8.00 apiece, and with the special tools which we have for them, perhaps a couple of hundred dollars more apiece for fitting them up.

The making of new brasses and a heavier set of wrist pins will make a greater weight.

8 March 1902—Wells diary (entry by Manly)

Mr. Manly makes first run on large engine in frame of Great Aerodrome, this being the first time engine has been started up since the

110

smash up on January 27th. Engine started up on first few turns of starting mechanism shaft, but bevel gear on starboard transmission shaft loosens up before engine gets fairly started and Mr. Manly immediately shuts off sparking current stopping engine. The bevel gears which are being used are the ones which were made originally for use with Balzer rotary cylinder engine which required that starboard and port gears should both be threaded left hand, while present engine requires that gears on starboard shafts should be right hand, and gears on port shaft be left hand. In order to save time and cost of making new gears for starboard shafts, which would also require that new shafts having right hand threads be made, Mr. Manly has put jamb nuts (right hand thread) on starboard shafts to keep gears on, but jamb nut on propeller shaft did not hold gear, apparently from nut not being *jammed hard against gear*. Nut will be jammed hard up against gear on Monday, and another run made, as it was six o'clock when the above accident stopped run. New type globular carbureter used in run.

10 March 1902—Wells diary (entry by Manly)

Bevel gear on starboard transmission shaft tightened up and nut jammed hard and sweated. Large tank carbureter connected to gas supply pipe.[51] Mr. Manly starts up engine with starting mechanism. Before engine gets fairly started, the starboard flywheel goes to smash, eleven of the twenty-four wire spokes breaking off short at the hub. Mr. Manly immediately stops engine before flywheel does any further damage. Upon inspection it is found that the bevel gear on the starboard transmission shaft has again loosened up, though the jamb nut has not moved. More seriously still the starting mechanism worm and worm wheel are found to be somewhat smashed up from outboard bearing of starting shaft having given way, allowing worm and worm wheel to get out of alignment. From same cause inboard thrust bearing of starting shaft has twisted and bent part of bedplate to which it is attached. Flywheels will be strengthened by putting in larger spokes, and all other parts immediately repaired. Flywheels had evidentally been strained in the serious smash up of January 27th.[52]

22 March 1902—Wells diary (entry by Manly)

The starting mechanism and flywheels being repaired, and the large engine reassembled in the frame of the large aerodrome, the transmission and propeller shafts were coupled up and everything gotten in

---

[51] This appears to be the Balzer type of carbureter.

[52] Actually 23–24 January (see page 109).

readiness for a trial at 4:40 p.m. Mr. Manly starts up engine unassisted, the engine starting readily upon his giving a few turns of the starting shaft to draw in the gas. Starboard flywheel writhes and buckles and appears very dangerous as though it would certainly go to pieces at even a moderate speed, and Mr. Manly therefore shuts off engine immediately before allowing it to speed up to examine flywheel. He finds one spoke very loose and another somewhat so, but decides to risk run, and immediately restarts engine. Starboard flywheel again writhes and twists, but seems to get no worse, at any rate, as engine is speeded up. However, before engine has speeded up to more than 200 rpm (a sound is heard) being as though the bevel gears are slipping, and it is found upon closer observation that the port propeller is apparently running only about one half as fast as the starboard one, which means that its gears *are* slipping. Mr. Manly immediately shuts down engine and finds that owing to workmen failing to put washer between port transmission shaft and engine shaft all of the strain from the gears has come on port 3 pronged bearing, buckling it out and thus allowing gear on transmission shaft to spring out of mesh with gear on propellar shaft. Teeth on gears are slightly bent and 3 pronged bearing seriously bent.

29 April 1902—Waste book entry by Langley

April 29 of last year, Mr. Manly reckoned that his new engine to develop 25 hp. would be done in June, that is June of 1901. The ten months have passed in incessant experiments and on the whole in improvements. A considerable part of this delay was represented by the failure of the contractors to deliver the steel shells and linear castings for the engine cylinders. These were received sometime in June, instead of January as promised. Another delay arose from the difficulty in applying the water jackets; but by the first of January of this year, 1902, the engine was substantially complete as regards the conditions under which it was undertaken. A little later in January an accident occurred due to defective crank brasses which caused the engine under trial to seriously injure four of the five cylinders, thus delaying the work a month from this cause.

The engine was first carried up and placed in the frame of the large aerodrome about February 15, 1902, and three trials have been made with it there, in each of which trials the transmission gears and bearings of the frame proved insufficient, thereby preventing the engine getting up to its full speed, and consequently not giving a full test as to the strength of the frame itself.

There have been many improvements which have brought the engine

112

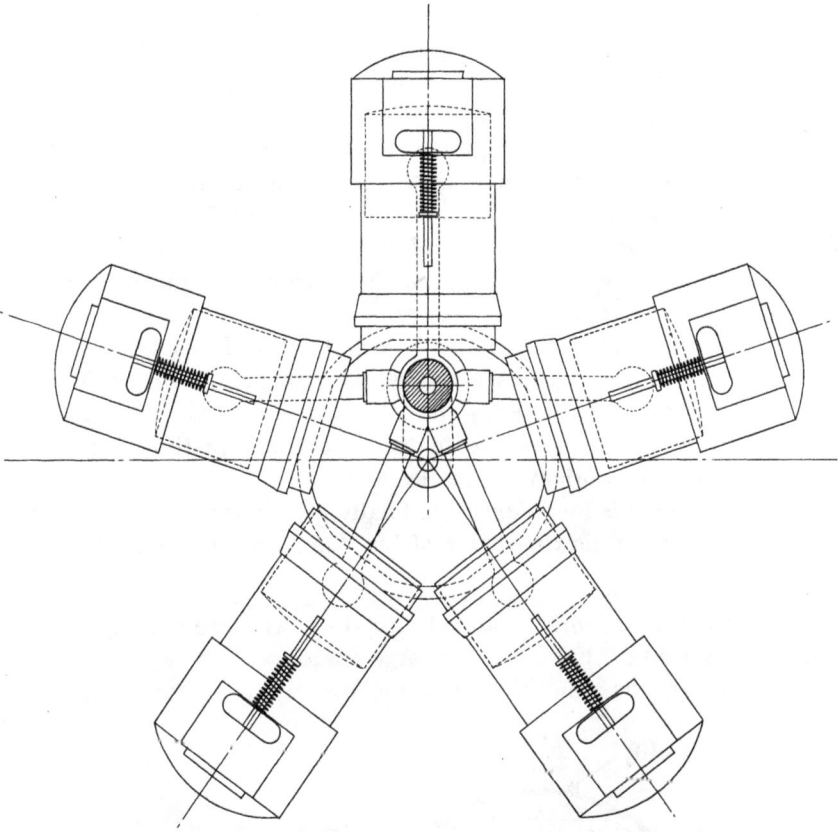

FIGURE 22.—Schematic drawing circa 1900 from Smithsonian Institution Archives illustrating master rod (top cylinder) with its bearing completely surrounding the crankshaft throw as designed by Manly, and Balzer-type of slipper bearings for the link rods (other cylinders). (Smithsonian photo A52558.)

above the 25 or 30 hp for which it was originally designed. Mr. Manly thinks the most important of these is a new crank bearing of his own invention which gives 4 times the former bearing surface on the crankshaft for each piston.[53] At the same time the new radiating condensers have been built and attached to the aerodrome frame. Almost every

---

[53] G. H. Corliss patented a master and link rod system in 1857 and built a stream pump utilizing this principle in 1875. Manly was forced to develop a similar system after greatly exceeding the horsepower for which the engine was designed. Balzer's slipper bearings (connecting rod to crankshaft) appear to have been satisfactory, however, up to 12 horsepower.

part of the guy wire system has been tested and strengthened. To diminish the shaking of the engine in the frame two flywheels have been applied, adding 20 pounds including the balance weights of 4 pounds. These have made the engine run, if not with ideal smoothness, yet so that the aerodrome with the engine at work can probably be mounted upon the [strengthened] uprights of the launching carriage with safety.

There have also been built 2 special "water friction" dynamometers [Figures 23, 24] for making the all-important determinations of the actual power given off at the brake by the large engine and its results with these have been most satisfactory.

The above refers to the machinists' work, but Reed and Darcy have been occupied, while at times assisting the machinists with small fittings for the frame, in completing the front part of the wings according to the drawings given elsewhere in this book, and in similar things which it is not easy to briefly summarize.

However, after this long delay, the finally greatly gratifying result is to be found in the following letter of Mr. Manly to me under date of April 28, 1902.

"In the shop test at which you and Captain Lewis were present Saturday, one of the five cylinders of the large engine was not working properly. However, the other four ran the two dynamometers, each of

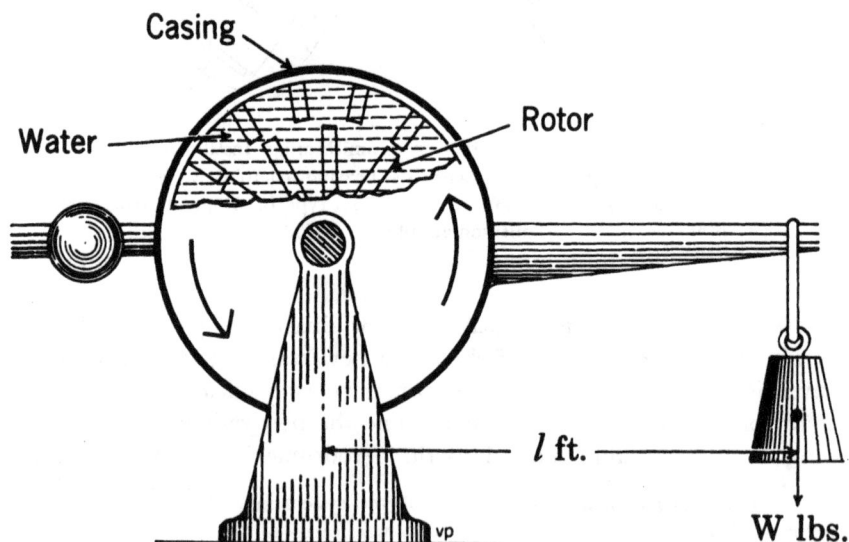

FIGURE 23.—Schematic drawing of hydraulic dynamometer by Harry T. Hart.
(Smithsonian photo A4517–A.)

FIGURE 24.—Water absorption (hydraulic) dynamometer used for testing Balzer-Manly engine. (Smithsonian photo A308.)

which has a lever arm of 13 inches, at a speed rising from 700 to over 1,000 rpm near the end of the run, at which point the coupling connecting the port dynamometer to the engine shaft was sheared off, the pull on each spring balance rising from 75 to over 100 pounds, the latter pull occurring just before and at the time when the coupling sheared off. The horsepower developed is calculated from the following formula:

$$\text{HP equals } 2\text{Pi } G \times A \times N/33,000,$$

where G equals the total pull on the two dynamometers in lbs.

A equals the length of the lever arm in feet
N equals number of revolutions per minute.

"In this test, where G equals 200 lbs.; A equals 13/12 ft.; and N equals 1,000 rpm we have from the formula, hp equals 41 plus.

"While I am not willing at the present time to make a definite statement as to the maximum power which the engine will develop, yet I consider it safe to now run the engine continuously (that is with safety as regards the engine itself) at a speed which renders 40 horsepower, though of course it is understood that I designed the engine with the view to having it furnish 25 horsepower, working under the conditions imposed by the aerodrome frame already constructed, and the system of gearing through which the large and low speed propellers are driven; and that the higher horsepowers of 40 or more are obtained at much higher speeds than I think would be possible to drive the propellers unless their size is somewhat reduced. It is also yet uncertain whether the frame of the aerodrome will be strong enough to hold the engine developing 25 horsepower, to say nothing of 40 horsepower, unless it is greatly strengthened; and in order to test this matter I placed the engine in the frame during the first part of the month of February, hoping to then make the test on this point; but in three successive tests the transmission gears and bearings proved insufficiently strong to stand the strain long enough for the engine to even reach full speed, so that I had to abandon these tests of the engine in the frame until I could complete the new and stronger transmission gears and bearings, which I am now doing, and which I expect to have complete within the next ten days.

"The actual weight of the engine, including all parts necessary to its operation, is 130 pounds, the engine not requiring any flywheels, so far as its mere running is concerned. However, in order to properly balance the moving parts, to reduce as far as possible the vibration, I have found it necessary to add two very specially constructed flywheels, including the balance weights, weighing approximately ten pounds each.[54] Though it is impossible to say definitely what will be the minimum amount of water required for properly cooling the engine when it is working in the frame and actually propelling the aerodrome through the air, yet from a careful perusal of similar engines on high speed automobiles, I have inferred that 25 pounds of water, rapidly circulated through the water jackets and the radiating condensers, will properly cool the engine in flight. This amount of water will, I think, keep the water jackets at an average temperature of about 95 degrees Centigrade, which I consider the best and most advantageous working temperature. With the engine working in the shop, and with no provision for cooling the water, but merely pumping it from a tank through the water jackets and back into the tank, 25 lbs. would not remain below the temperature of 95 degrees Centigrade more than for 3 or 4 minutes; but since the aerodrome should certainly be launched within 3 minutes after starting up the engine, I have no great fear of any serious trouble from the overheating of the engine cylinders.

"The flying weight of the engine, including all accessories, I think will come very close to 200 pounds, of which 130 pounds is for the actual engine itself, 20 pounds for the two flywheels, 25 pounds for the cooling water, 17 pounds for the condenser, 1 pound for the pump, 3 pounds for the sparking coil, 9 pounds for the sparking dynamo or battery, besides a few minor water connections, electrical wires, etc." [55]

17 June 1902—Manly to Langley both in Washington, D.C. (in part)

The new five cylinder engine was completed during the first week of January, 1902, and since that time numerous tests of it have been made, using the water controlled dynamometers which were especially invented and constructed for it.[56] The objects of these tests have been, (a) to determine the brake horsepower developed when the engine is working at its best and also when under conditions such as may possibly occur while the engine is driving the aerodrome through the air, when the carbureter may not give exactly the correct mixture of gases, the time of the electric spark may not be quite correctly adjusted, or one or more cylinders may not be quite correctly adjusted, or one or more cylinders may not furnish power, due to various causes. (b) To improve

---

[54] Had the engine been left as a rotary, there would have been no vibration problems so that the 20 pound weight of the flywheels could have been eliminated.

[55] Had the engine been left as a rotary, perhaps with finned cylinders, 43 "cooling" pounds would have been saved with a slight decrease in horsepower due to the windage of the rotating cylinders.

[56] Water absorption dynamometers were used as early as 1865.

382-902 O · 71 · 9

Figure 25.—Balzer-type carbureter Now on exhibit at the Smithsonian Institution. (Smithsonian photo A18081.)

the carbureter [Figure 25] which has been especially invented and constructed for the engine, and to render it as nearly absolutely reliable as possible under varying conditions of temperature and wind velocity.[57] (c) To reduce to a minimum the vibration due to unbalanced reciprocating parts and to reverse torque, by adjustments of the balance weights and by the reduction of the inertia of the moving parts.[58]

The general results of these tests were, (a) that at 950 rpm and with all accessories of the engine working properly, the dynamometers recorded a pull of 265 pounds on a 13 inch lever, which is equivalent to 51 brake horsepower, that at 875 rpm the engine gave 45 bhp, that at 800 rpm the engine gave 40 hp, and that at 750 rpm and with one cylinder not working, the engine gave 28 bhp. (b) The vibration has been reduced to a point where it appears reasonable to expect that it will not cause any serious strains in the frame of the aerodrome, or any great inconvenience to the aeronaut. I hope to be able to still further reduce

---

[57] This was similar to the original Balzer carbureter, but enlarged to accommodate the enlarged cylinders of the "new" engine.

[58] Had the engine been left as a rotary, these problems would not have occurred.

118

the vibration as soon as the engine is working the frame, where I can study more minutely the effects of different changes I propose making. (c) The carbureter has been steadily improved in its reliability and I expect to have it thoroughly satisfactory very soon after I get the engine working in the frame, where I can utilize the currents of air from the large propellers to study the effects of wind on it.

The engine proper complete weighs 125 pounds, or a little less than 2½ pounds per horsepower, if we take as a basis the power developed under perfect working conditions, which is the custom of all builders of engines for such purposes. Including cooling water, pump, condenser, sparking coil, batteries, carbureter, tanks and all such accessories necessary to the proper working of the engine, it weighs just 200 pounds, or slightly less than 4 pounds per brake horsepower for its "flying weight."

A new type of crank bearing, to enable the five piston rods to work cn a single crank and at the same time to give each one its full crank pin bearing, has been invented and constructed, and has been used in all of the tests since March, and has proved to be absolutely perfect, solving completely the very difficult problem of proper lubrication, which had given me the greatest concern since the beginning of the construction of the engine.

3 July 1902—Manly in Washington, D.C., to Langley in Europe (in part)

I now have the large engine working in the aerodrome frame and delivering the power of [to] the propellers through the newly designed and constructed transmission shafts, gears, etc., and everything so far has worked very well. The vibration of the engine is very small indeed considering the power developed but it is not so small as I wish it to be, and I am now just starting experiments running the engine in the frame, as a result of which I hope to be able to reduce the vibration still further.

18 July 1902—Manly in Washington, D.C., to Langley in Europe (in part)

A few minutes after writing to you on July third, I started up the large engine in the frame to begin the measurements of the actual thrust or "lift." [59] The engine had been working about three minutes at 550 revolutions and driving the 2½ meter unit pitch propellers and developing a thrust of 280 pounds, when I noticed that the top cylinder was

---

[59] This was accomplished by securing the frame to a carriage mounted on a track. The thrust developed by the propellers was measured by a spring scale.

getting almost red hot. I immediately shut down the engine and found that the cooling water supply for the top cylinder had, in some unexplained way, gotten choked off, and upon removing the top cylinder, found that the excessive heat had caused some of the brazed joints to come loose, which necessitated the removal of the jacket on the top cylinder in order to repair the damage. The extra cylinders not being yet complete, there have, of course, been no further tests on the engine working in the frame since that time; but I am now completing the repairs on the top cylinder and expect to have the engine working again in the frame and on the launching car during the early part of next week.

1 August 1902—Manly in Washington, D.C., to Langley in Europe (in part)

Since my letter of July 18th, I have completed the repairs to the top cylinder which was injured in the previous run, and have also completed one of the extra cylinders and have had the engine again working in the frame on the launching car. I regret to say, however, that on Monday, July 28th, while the engine was running in the frame, the port propeller suddenly twisted off at the hub but fortunately the broken part flew in the direction of the floor and did not injure the frame. The large bevel gear on the port propeller shaft had four teeth broken out of it and, of course, requiring a new gear. The repairs, however, are now about completed and I expect to make another run tomorrow.

15 August 1902—Manly in Washington, D.C., to Langley in Europe (in part)

I am pleased to be able to say that after considerable delays, caused by first one part and then another of the frame breaking, I now have the engine working regularly in the aerodrome frame and have been letting it run up as high as thirty-five brake horsepower. Quite a bit of the delay has been due to the propellers breaking under the strain of the work, but I am now building some new and stronger ones, all of the ones on hand having gone to pieces. All of the work is progressing in a satisfactory manner, except for continual set-backs due to various causes to which the work, as ever, has been particularly subject.

18 August 1902—Langley in Germany to Manly in Washington, D.C.

I have I think, answered your previous letter of July 18, and have now to acknowledge yours of August 1st.

The injury to the propeller and bevel gear is only in the normal course of accidents. Perhaps we ought to be glad rather than sorry that they have happened in the shop instead of a thousand feet above it! But as the time for flight draws very near I confess my anxieties, for the incalculable play of what is all but chance, increase. I admit that I feel almost a shrinking from the time of trial which I suppose is now so near.

29 August 1902—Manly in Washington, D.C., to Langley in Europe (in part)

I have to acknowledge with thanks your very kind letter of August 18th from Karlsbad, where I am pleased to note that you then were, and the visit to which I trust has been of much pleasure and benefit to you.

Since my letter of August 15th I have been making a series of experiments with the engine working in the frame under artificially produced air drafts acting on the carbureter, to imitate as far as possible the actual conditions under which the carbureter will work when the aerodrome is in flight, and to determine beforehand, as far as possible, the changes in adjustment that the carbureter will require in the few seconds of *greatly changed conditions* when the aerodrome starts from a position of rest and is rapidly accelerated in its travel to the end of the track where it becomes free in the air. This question of the change of conditions seriously affecting the carbureter, and consequently the working of the engine, is the cause of more anxiety to me than anything else which I anticipate may happen to cause a failure at the first launching of the machine, and I shall not feel that we are sufficiently prepared for the first trial until I can obtain more information, than I have yet been able to do, with the machine working under conditions artificially produced and as nearly similar as possible to those to be actually met.

9 September 1902—Langley in London to Manly in Washington, D.C.

I have your letter of the 29th and am not surprised that my pessimistic forecast as to the time has been partly justified. I think you are very prudent to imitate the actual conditions under which the carbureter will work when the aerodrome is in flight, in its first few critical seconds.

I have changed my steamer and do not expect to sail now until the 25th hoping to reach Boston on October 3rd. With goodwill and sympathy in your disappointments.

17 September 1902—Manly in Washington, D.C., to Langley in Boston (in part)

The continual breakage of the propellers, which was totally unexpected, as I had thought for a year or more that the propellers we had on hand would be amply strong for the work expected of them, has already delayed the work at least four or six weeks and has completely upset all of my calculations as to when I would be ready to start the houseboat with everything on board down the River, and until I overcome this trouble with the propellers, I can give no idea of when the aerodrome will be ready for trial. However, I am getting all of the other work in shape as rapidly as possible with the expectation of starting down the River at the earliest possible time, so that I trust you will not worry regarding the delays which are now being experienced.

26 September 1902—Manly in Washington, D.C., to Langley in Boston (in part)

Since my letter of September 17th I have been continuing the tests with the engine working in the frame and on September 19th met with another serious breakdown. This time the propeller shafts which had been in use for sometime and which had withstood all the usual strains which had heretofore broken the propellers, twisted and buckled under the strain of driving the propellers, the buckling and twisting being so serious as to require the construction of new shafts. However, I have gotten the new shafts complete and am just now putting them in the frame and expect to have everything in working order again tomorrow.

10 November 1902—Langley in Washington, D.C., to Captain I. N. Lewis, Fort Casey, Washington (in part)

I tell you privately that the engine for which we owe so much to Mr. Manly is finally showing itself perhaps the best anywhere at present, for he reports it running at forty horsepower, while weighing, with cooling water and every accessory, about two hundred pounds, though part even of this weight is due to flywheels and weights (on the spokes of the flywheels) required by the light frame. Working on the bench, including cooling water, its weight is less.

Everything is ready, and were there still time this season, a flight would be made, but I do not expect one until after the ice has gone; then I, who has never known any great initiatory trial without some mischance, look for what I call our "first smash." When every human care has been taken, there remains the element of the unknown. There may well be something that forethought has not provided for, and I ex-

122

pect it and fear it, but excepting for the fact that a human life is now in question, I could make it without fear at all.

4 January 1903—Langley memorandum

Mr. Manly says in substance—

"Since December I have been prepared to make a flight. The whole machine including the sustaining surfaces, and seat, and the whole of the houseboat and apparatus for launching, is ready to the last degree, except those things which are necessarily left to the day or two proceeding the actual trial. In particular, the engine is actually delivering (after the deductions from the use of the bevel gears) 45 brake hp at the propellers. This, however, still demands an incessant personal attention, though not so imperatively as formerly, since it may run fifteen minutes without attention, but may also run less, or it may stop altogether. Each month the thing grows more under control, but I can never expect to be free from anxiety as to what will happen in the first few seconds of the launch. That over, and the machine once in the air, if the engine works satisfactorily at the end of the first ten seconds, I have no fear of its not continuing.

"I have improved the carbureter and other points until I have had it running without any personal interference for fifteen or twenty minutes, developing the same amount. The whole question, however, (now that the other things have been made so nearly right) is that of the supply of gas from the carbureter. There is no certainty that it will work well or ill, or work at all without my personal attention. To put it in such a condition that it will work under any conditions or with another man, requires still an indefinite time. I will not guarantee that three months will do this.

"It is in this work that the large staff of men is still employed, and in the building of the three extra cylinders which you have wished to have; so that with the three on hand belonging to the Smithsonian Institution, there may be at any time more cylinders than enough to reconstruct the present engine."

23 March 1903—Manly to Langley both in Washington, D.C.

I have your letter of this date. Your understanding as to the condition of the work is correct.

I add that I have repeatedly had the engine running in its actual position on the frame driving the 2½ meter propellers, with a power of over 45 brake horse, with entire smoothness,—the engine running at 745

FIGURE 26.—Manly (in aviator's car) and Reed (below with straw hat) making adjustments to partially assembled aerodrome frame in place on its catapult during the latter part of September 1903. (Smithsonian photo A18782.)

revolutions per minute, and the two propellers at 575, developing jointly a thrust of over 300 lbs.

Every part of the aerodrome and guys has been minutely tested. The carbureter works so that I am not apprehensive of any failure of the

first rush, and I am prepared to risk myself with it in actual flight, as soon as the final adjustments, balancing, etc., are made.

I may add that the engine proper, including all necessary working parts, and comprising everything that is intrinsically a part of it, weighs 120 lbs., and develops on test 52 brake horsepower, *or at the rate of 1.05 kilograms per brake horsepower.*

125

FIGURE 28.—Langley aerodrome poised on its catapult-houseboat during the latter part of September 1903. (Smithsonian photo A18840.)

On 7 October and 8 December 1903 two unsuccessful attempts were made to launch the aerodrome. In each case the airframe suffered extensive damage from the moment of launching, however, the engine worked perfectly, and was recovered from the bottom of the Potomac River after each trial in undamaged condition. Its future was doomed, however, because of the aerodrome's failures.

The engine was separated from the airframe in order to prepare it for the St. Louis Exposition contest and has, subsequently, maintained its own identity as the crowning achievement of the entire aerodromic program. It is exhibited separately at the Smithsonian Institution; recently a dummy reproduction of it has been installed in the aerodrome.

23 May 1904—Manly to Langley both in Washington, D.C.

Referring to our conversation in the early part of April when I mentioned the subject of the entrance of the large engine in the competition for the prize for light weight motors at the St. Louis Exposition, I now beg to again bring the matter to your attention.

126

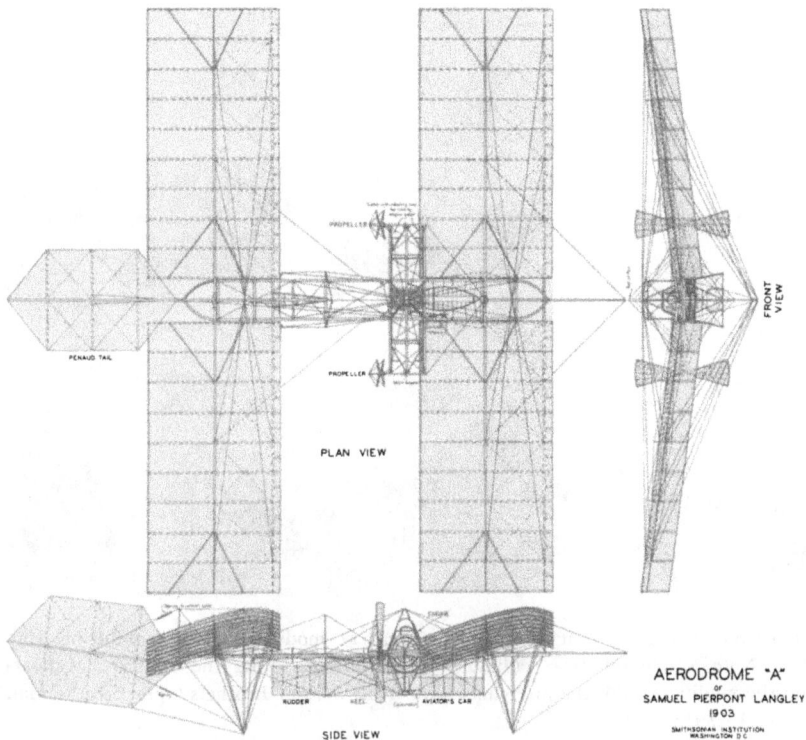

FIGURE 29.—Three-view drawing of Langley aerodrome in its 1903 configuration. (Smithsonian photo A38167.)

The prize is provided for under Section II (Motors for Airships or Dirigible Balloons) of the rules governing the secondary contests, which is as follows:

"A first prize of Twenty-five Hundred Dollars ($2,500.00) and a second prize of One Thousand Dollars ($1,000.00) are offered for the airship motors other than the exact machine winning the grand prize, having the least weight and greatest efficiency in proportion to their power."

"The first test will cover one hour's run to determine power, and the second test a continuous run of ten hours for ascertaining the reliability and durability of the apparatus."

As the motor winning this prize will no doubt be considered the lightest per horsepower in the world, and as I think it very certain that no one else has one so light as this one which I have invented and

FIGURE 30.—Glenn H. Curtiss in aviator's car of modified aerodrome during May 1914. Note automobile-type radiator and carbureter. Note the addition of floats and the modification of the propellers toward the Wright Brothers-type. (Smithsonian photo A52394.)

built, I should regret it very much if an inferior construction were permitted to receive the credit which seems to belong here.

I have estimated that the expense of making the tests at St. Louis (including transportation and subsistence for myself and a machinist and the wages of a machinist) will be something like five hundred dollars. This I am prepared to bear personally if the permission is granted me to enter the engine in the contest.

It appears to me that the interest of the aerodromic work and of the Institution itself would be furthered by an exhibition of what has been accomplished and I therefore beg to ask your permission to enter the engine in the competition.

The idea of entering the engine in these contests had not occurred to me until suggested and urged by several men whose opinions in such matters are of importance.[60]

---

[60] Permission was granted and money was allotted to exhibit the engine and enter it in the contest; however, the following telegram was received from the Exposition, "On account of lack of competition engine tests abandoned."

As a result of an agreement between Secretary Walcott of the Smithsonian Institution and Glenn H. Curtiss, the last attempts to power the Aerodrome model A with its original engine were made in April 1914.

The machine was shipped to Curtiss at Hammondsport, N.Y. in April. Dr. Zahm, the Recorder of the Langley Aerodynamical Laboratory and expert witness for Curtiss in the patent litigation [with the Wright Brothers], was at Hammondsport as official representative of the Smithsonian Institution during the time the machine was being reconstructed and tested. In the reconstruction the machine was changed from what it was in 1903 in a number of particulars as given in Dr. Wright's list of differences which appears later in this paper. On the 28th of May and the 2d of June, 1914, attempts to fly were made. After acquiring speed by running on hydroplane floats on the surface of Lake Keuka the machine lifted into the air several different times. The longest time off the water with the Langley motor was approximately five seconds. Dr. Zahm stated that "it was apparent that owing to the great weight which had been given to the structure by adding the floats it was necessary to increase the propeller thrust." So no further attempts were made to fly with the Langley 52 HP engine.[61]

Stage four marked the engine's highest performance peak and assured it an undisputed title of the most advanced and most powerful airplane engine in the world at the turn of the century.

------

[61] C. G. Abbot, "The 1914 Tests of the Langley 'Aerodrome'" *Smithsonian Miscellaneous Collections* (Washington: Smithsonian Institution), vol. 103, no. 8, pp. 1–2.

Chapter 7

Evaluation of the Balzer-Manly Aero Engine

*I*n addition to the Balzer-Manly aero engine, there are two other full
size gasoline engines on display in the National Air and Space
Museum which first powered aircraft in 1903. A comparison of these
engines reveals the state of the art at the turn of the century, and the
preeminence of the Balzer-Manly engine.

The Wright Brothers Engine of 1903 [62]

The heaviest of these engines for its horsepower (approximately 16
lbs for each hp) was the one Orville and Wilbur Wright designed
themselves and built with the help of their machinist, Charles E. Taylor in the remarkably short time of three months.

They began to build it in December 1902, and the first tests were run
on February 12, 1903. On the 13th dripping gasoline caused the bearings to freeze, and this broke the engine body and frame. It was necessary to order a new aluminum casting which was received on April 20,
1903. The rebuilt motor was shop tested in May. In a description of the
motor by Wilbur Wright dated February 28, 1903, he had this to say:

We recently built a four-cylinder gasoline engine with 4″ piston and 4″ stroke,
to see how powerful it would be, and what it would weigh. At 670 revolutions per
min. it developed 8½ horsepower, brake test. By speeding it up to 1,000 rev. we
will easily get 11 horsepower and possibly a little more at still higher speed, though
the increase is not in exact proportion to the increase in number of revolutions.
The weight including the 30-pound flywheel is 140 lbs.

---

[62] ROBERT B. MEYER, JR., "Three Famous Early Aero Engines" *Annual Report of
the Board of Regents of the Smithsonian Institution, 1961,* (Washington: Smithsonian Institution) pp. 357–371.

A description of the rebuilt motor by Orville Wright dated 28 June, 1903, follows: "Since putting in heavier springs to actuate the valves on our engine we have increased its power to nearly 16 horsepower, and at the same time reduced the amount of gasoline consumed per hour to about one half of what it was before."

By November 5, 1903, the engine had been tested in the Wrights' first powered airplane, the "Kitty Hawk Flyer." Considerable trouble was experienced with the propeller shafts. Finally, new ones had to be made, and so the engine did not become successfully airborne until December 17, 1903.

A detailed description of the motor follows. It consists of quotations from *The Papers of Wilbur and Orville Wright,* edited by Marvin W. McFarland.

This historic motor is described by Orville Wright in an undated typewritten memorandum among the Wright papers in the Library of Congress: The motor used in the first flights at Kitty Hawk, N. C., on December 17, 1903, had (four) horizonal cylinders of 4-inch bore and 4-inch stroke. The ignition was by low-tension magneto with make-and-break spark. The boxes inclosing the intake and exhaust valves had neither water jackets nor radiating fins, so that after a few minutes' run the valves and valve boxes became red hot. There was no float-feed carbureter. The gasoline was fed to the motor by gravity in a constant stream and was vaporized by running over a large heated surface of the water jacket of the cylinders. Due to the preheating of the air by the water jacket and the red-hot valves and boxes, the air greatly expanded before entering the cylinders. As a result, in a few minutes' time, the power dropped to less than 75 percent of what it was on cranking the motor.

*   *   *   *   *

The crankcase and water jacket were cast in a single block of aluminum alloy. The crankshaft was made from a block of machine steel 1⅝ inches thick and had five babbitted main bearings. A 15-inch, 26-pound flywheel was attached to the rear end of the shaft. A chain drive on the front end drove the camshaft, which operated the breaker arms and exhaust valves. A boxwood idler, 1¼ inches in diameter, without flanges, created tension on the chain.

The valve heads were made of cast iron. The stems were of steel. The intake valves operated automatically. Neither the cylinders nor the pistons were ground. The connecting rods were seamless steel tubes screwed into brass big ends.

The motor was started with the aid of a dry-battery coil box. After starting, ignition was provided by a low-tension magneto, friction-driven by the flywheel. This magneto—permanent horseshoe magnets with exciting coils—weighed 18 pounds. Insulated ignition electrodes in the cylinder heads were connected by a strap of copper. The speed of the motor was regulated on the ground by retarding the spark. A small lever on the leg of the motor controlled the timing of the spark by altering the position of the camshaft. There was no way to regulate the speed of the motor in flight.

Lubrication was supplied to the cylinders by a small oil pump driven by a worm gear on the camshaft. No pump was used in the cooling system. The vertical sheet-steel radiator was attached to the central forward upright. Gas feed was controlled by a metering valve, not adjustable during flight. A shutoff valve, made from an ordinary gaslight pet cock, was placed conveniently near the operator. The fuel tank had a capacity of 0.4 gallon. The fuel line was copper.

The weight of the 1903 engine is given as 161 pounds dry in Orville Wright's letter to Charles L. Lawrance, November 15, 1928, or 179 pounds with magneto. Complete with magneto, radiator, tank, water, fuel, tubing, and accessories, the powerplant weighed a little over 200 pounds.

Additional information about this engine was furnished by Charles E. Taylor in an article that appeared in the May 1928 issue of the journal Slipstream.[63] *A partial quotation follows:*

Orv and Will then asked me to help them build the motor for their first power-driven machine. They had a little workshop where they built and repaired bicycles at 1927 West Third Street. As I recall we first hit upon the idea of an air-cooled motor but we decided after some figuring that it would weigh more per horsepower than a water-cooled type so we settled upon the latter. I do not know but that if we could have secured the light alloys available today we would have gone ahead with the air-cooled job.

The first thing we did as an experiment was to construct a sort of skeleton model in order that we might watch the functioning of the various vital parts before venturing with anything more substantial. Orv and Will were pretty thorough that way—they wouldn't take anything for granted but worked everything out to a practical solution without too much haste. I think that had a lot to do with their later success.

When we had the skeleton motor set up we hooked it to our shop power, smeared the cylinders with a paint brush dipped in oil and watched the various parts in action. It looked good so we went ahead immediately with the construction of a four cylinder engine. I cut the crankshaft from a solid block of steel weighing over a hundred pounds. When finished it weighed about 19 pounds. We didn't have spark plugs but used the old "make and break" system of ignition. The gas was led in and made to spread over the chamber above the heated water jackets and this immediately vaporized it. Of course, we had real gasoline in that day—fully 76 proof and you could count on it going into action at the least excuse.

The cylinders of that first motor were made of gray iron as were the

---

[63] Fred Marshall, "Building the Original Wright Motor," *Slipstream* (May 1928).

pistons. As I recall those cylinders were from ⅛ inch to ³/₁₆ inch in thickness. So far as I know that was the first four cylinder engine ever built. The automobile manufacturers were out of the picture then and the Oldsmobile firm was the only one I was familiar with at that time. We tried to get a motor built there but they couldn't make one near the low weight we wanted. The old one-lunger auto engines of that day really weighed more than our entire flying machine with the first motor installed.

When the engine was ready for block test we rigged up a connection with natural gas, put on a resistance fan and made several block runs in this manner. Later we used gasoline fuel and found the motor would run satisfactorily. That first motor developed around 18 h.p. and weighed around 190 pounds. We were all highly pleased at being able to hold down the weight to this figure but a short time afterward we built another motor that produced around 45 h.p. and which weighed about the same as the first one.

When we installed the first motor in the original machine it lay on its side to right of the pilot and in such a position that the pilot's weight partially offset that of the motor. The radiator was made from speaking tubes flattened to reduce the capacity.

Yes, I must admit there wasn't much to that first motor—no car-- bureter, no spark plugs, not much of anything but cylinders, pistons and connecting rods, but it worked.

SPECIFICATIONS

Cylinders	— 4 horizontal in-line
Cooling	— Water
Carburetion	— Surface type—no float
Ignition	— Low-tension magneto with make-and-break spark
Horsepower	— 12.05 at 1,090 r.p.m.
Bore and stroke	— 4 x 4 in.
Displacement	— 201.1 cu. in.
Dimensions	— 13⅝ in. high x 23½₃₂ in. wide x 30¹¹/₁₆ in. long
Weight	— Slightly over 200 pounds including cooling water.
Weight/h.p. ratio	— Approximately 16.6 lb. per h.p.
Country of manufacture	— U.S.A.

133

382-902 O - 71 - 10

On 7 June 1903 Wilbur Wright wrote to George A. Spratt: [64]

"About Christmastime we began the construction of the motor, which is of four cylinders, four-inch bore and four-inch stroke. We had estimated that we would require a little over eight horsepower to carry our weight of 625 lbs. of machine and man. At this weight we would be limited to two hundred lbs. for our motor. Our motor on completion turned out to be a very pleasant surprise. Instead of eight horsepower, for which we hoped but hardly expected, it has given us 13 [non-continuous] horsepower on the brake, with a [dry] weight of only 150 lbs. in the motor."

Although the 1903 Wright brothers' motor was heavier for the horsepower it delivered than those of Santos Dumont or Professor Langley (respectively two and four times as heavy), it nevertheless fulfilled its function. On April 12, 1911, Orville Wright wrote: "We look upon reliability in running as of much more importance than lightness of weight in aeroplane motors. We attempt to design our flyers of such efficiency that extremely light motors are not needed."

Since the Wright brothers did not have the wealth of Santos Dumont or the Government grant of Langley, it was necessary for them to build their own engines [Figures 31–33]. It therefore had to be of practical and simple design. A logical procedure was to adapt the automobile engine to the requirements of the airplane, which is what they did.

The next heaviest of these engines for its horsepower (approximately (8 lbs for each hp) was the French designed and built Clement motor (made by Adolphe Clement, who later founded the famous Clement-Bayard firm). It powered the Brazilian Santos Dumont's airship No. 9 during the summer of 1903. To quote from his book, My Air-ships: [65]

I determined to build a small airship runabout for my pleasure and convenience only. . . . So I built my number 9, the smallest of possible dirigibles, yet very practical indeed. As originally constructed, its balloon capacity was but 7,770 cubic feet, permitting me to take up less than 66 pounds of ballast; and thus I navigated it for weeks, without inconvenience. Even when I enlarged its balloon to 9,218 cubic feet, the balloon of my number 6, in which I won the Deutsch Prize, would have made almost three of it, while that of my Omnibus is fully eight times its size. As I have already stated, its 3 horsepower Clement motor

---

[64] MEYER, op. cit., p. 367. See also MARVIN W. McFARLAND, Editor, *The Papers of Wilbur and Orville Wright* (New York: McGraw-Hill Book Company, Inc., 1953), vol. 1, p. 313.

[65] A. SANTOS-DUMONT, *My Air-Ships* (New York: The Century Co., 1904), p. 313.

FIGURE 31.—Wright Brothers engine. Left front view showing automatic intake valves, rocker-arm actuated exhaust valves, fuel induction system, timing chain, and spark advance lever. (Smithsonian photo A41898–A.)

weighs but 26½ pounds. With such a motor one cannot expect great speed; nevertheless, this handy little runabout takes me over the Bois [Paris] at between 12 and 15 miles per hour, and this notwithstanding its egg-shaped form, which would seemingly be little calculated for cutting the air.

Further information is given in "The New Santos-Dumont Airships," by the Paris correspondent of the Scientific American, *11 July 1903:* [66]

The new Clement gasoline motor used on the number 9 has proved especially satisfactory. The little motor with its cylinders joined in the form of a V to a round aluminum crank box seems like a toy and weighs but 26½ pounds, although it will develop 3 horsepower. The weight per horsepower (8.8 pounds), the smallest that has yet been reached, is the result of long experience in racing cars, where weight must be cut down to a minimum. Current for the spark is supplied by a battery and induction coil of the motor-bicycle pattern. The motor is connected through a light friction clutch to the long shaft which passes back to the propeller. A bicycle wheel with a heavy rim [without tire]

[66] Volume 89, no. 2, p. 25.

FIGURE 32.—Wright Brothers engine. Underside view showing flywheel, oil pump, exhaust valve camshaft, rocker arms, and valve springs, and ignition system camshaft. (Smithsonian photo A41898–C.)

forms the flywheel and lies next to the motor. . . . An air-bag of 60 cubic yards lies along the inside of the ballon at the bottom, forming a pocket which can be filled out with air by a fan [blower] mounted on the motor shaft. The balloon is [therefore] always kept in shape as the gas escapes.

SPECIFICATIONS [67]

Cylinders	— 2 arranged in the form of a V.
Cooling	— Air.
Carburetion	— Automobile-type carbureter
Ignition	— Battery, induction coil, spark plug (high-tension)
Horsepower	— 3
Bore and stroke	— 2¼ x 2¾ in.
Displacement	— 21.8 cu. in.

[67] MEYER, op. cit., pp. 358–359.

FIGURE 33.—Wright Brothers engine. Right rear view as mounted in the airplane, showing the flywheel, magneto, propeller drive chains, automatic intake valve springs, and open-ended can surface-type carbureter. (Smithsonian photo A38388.)

Dimensions   — 17 in. high x 9½ in. wide x 9 in. long
Weight   — 26½ lb
Weight/hp ratio   — 8.8 lb. per hp.
Country of manufacture — France.

The Clement engine had two tasks to perform: the propulsion of a lighter-than-air craft, and the operation of a blower (fan) to aid in maintaining the rigidity and therefore the structural integrity of the dirigible's envelope (balloon) .

As Santos Dumont stated above, this motor would propel his diminutive airship up to 15 mph. Forcing it much beyond this speed would not have been practical because of the envelope's great resistance to the passage of the air. If a considerably more powerful engine had been installed, it would have weighed so much that little or no ballast could have been carried. This would have prevented safe aerial navigation.

The blower, as mentioned above, merely forced air under low pressure into a flexible compartment on the underside of the gas bag. This compensated for any reduction in stiffness of the airship's envelope due to a loss of lifting gas caused by leakage or purposeful releasing of the

137

FIGURE 34.—Clement engine. Rear view showing cylinders, valve mechanisms, flywheel, clutch, and blower. Now on exhibit at the Smithsonian Institution. (Smithsonian photo A46816–B.)

FIGURE 35.—Clement engine. Left side showing the left cylinder and its valve mechanism, spark-timing system, flywheel, clutch, and blower. Now on exhibit at the Smithsonian Institution. (Smithsonian photo A46816–A.)

FIGURE 36.—Clement engine. Right side showing the right cylinder and its valve mechanism, spark-timing system, carbureter, clutch, and flywheel. Now on exhibit at the Smithsonian Institution. (Smithsonian photo A46816.)

140

gas. Probably only a fraction of one horsepower was needed for this purpose.

This particular engine [Figures 34–36] was apparently designed for the Clement Autocyclette motorcycle which was sold in 1903. However, its light weight and reasonably good weight/power ratio made it an ideal engine for the diminutive airship.

The Balzer-Manly Engine of 1903

The lightest of these engines for its horsepower (approximately 4 lbs per hp) was the engine which is the subject of this book. Manly describes it in the following excerpts from, "The Langley Memoir on Mechanical Flight" [68] *now out of print and largely unavailable.*

The main requirement in an engine for an aerodrome—aside from reliability and smoothness of operation, which are necessary in an engine for any kind of locomotion—is that it shall develop the greatest amount of power for the least weight. It is, therefore, desirable to reduce the weight and number of parts of the engine to the very minimum, so far as this can be done without sacrificing reliability and smoothness of running. Furthermore, since the strongest metal for its weight is steel, and since the greatest strength of steel is utilized when the stress acting on it is one of tension, it is advisable to design the engine so that parts which sustain the greatest strains shall be of steel and, as far as possible, meet with strains which are purely tensional ones.

In designing the new engine for the large aerodrome it was, therefore, planned to make it entirely of steel, as far as this was possible. The only parts which were not of steel were the bronze bushings for the bearings, the cast-iron pistons, and cast-iron liners of the cylinders. Previous experience had shown that, while it is possible to use a cast-iron piston in a steel cylinder or even a steel piston in a steel cylinder, provided the lubrication be kept exactly adjusted, yet the proper lubrication of the piston and cylinder of a gas engine is difficult under the most favorable conditions, owing to the fact that excessive lubrication causes trouble from the surplus oil interfering with the sparking apparatus. It was, therefore, determined not to risk serious trouble by attempting to have the pistons bear directly on the steel walls of the cylinders.

* * * * *

[68] *Smithsonian Contributions to Knowledge*, vol. 27, no. 3, pp. 234–246.

FIGURE 37.—Balzer-Manly engine, exhaust side. Now on exhibit at the Smithsonian Institution. (Smithsonian photo A54409.)

142

The engine cylinders consisted primarily of a main outer shell of steel one-sixteenth of an inch thick, near the bottom of which was screwed and brazed a suitable flange, by which it was bolted to the supporting drum or crank chamber. These shells, which were seamless, with the heads formed integral, were designed to be of sufficient strength to withstand the force of the explosion in them, and, in order to provide a suitable wearing surface for the piston, a cast-iron liner one-sixteenth of an inch thick was carefully shrunk into them. Entering the side of the cylinder near the top, was the combustion chamber, machined out of a solid steel forging, which also formed the port which entered the cylinder and was fastened to it by brazing. The water jackets, which were formed of sheet steel .020 inch thick, were also fastened to the cylinder by brazing.

* * * * *

The engine consists primarily of a single crankshaft provided with a single crank pin, the shaft having bearings in a drum which consists essentially of two heads. Arranged around the crankshaft and attached at equidistant points of the drum are five cylinders. Mounted on the port side of the crankshaft and close to the crank arm is a small gear, which through suitable gears mounted on the port head of the drum drives a double-pointed cam which has a bearing on the exterior of the hub of the drum. The ratio of these gears is such that the cam is driven at one-quarter the speed of the crankshaft, and in the reverse direction. Mounted on the exterior side of the port head of the drum are five punch rods, the upper ends of which are within a sixty-fourth of an inch of being in contact with the exhaust-valve stems of the cylinders, and on the lower end of these rods are hardened-steel rollers which rest on the double-pointed cam—this one cam thus serving to operate the exhaust valves of all five of the cylinders. The port head of the drum is connected to the port bed plate, by which it is supported, by means of a flanged bushing in which are formed tongues and grooves which fit into corresponding grooves and tongues formed in the hub of the drum, it being necessary to have a certain amount of space between this bed plate and the head of the drum to provide room for the exhaust-valve cam and its co-acting punch rods. The starboard bed plate is fastened to the starboard head of the drum by bolts which draw the web of the bed plate against the face of the drum. The sparking gears are driven by means of a gear formed on a sleeve which telescopes over the hub of the starboard drum, and has a bearing thereon, the end of the sleeve terminating in a ring which is fastened to the crankshaft.

Since the five connecting rods must center on the one crank pin, the

143

FIGURE 38.—Balzer-Manly engine, ignition side. Now on exhibit at the Smithsonian
Institution. (Smithsonian photo A49990–B.)

144

FIGURE 39.—Balzer-Manly engine, exhaust side showing starting crank, piston, and water radiator. Formerly exhibited at the Smithsonian Institution. (Smithsonian photo A26484.)

145

bronze shoes in which they terminate can occupy only a portion of the circumference of the pin, and with the relative proportions which here existed between the length of a stroke of crank and the length of the connecting rod, the circumferential width of the connecting-rod shoes was slightly less than sixty degrees, thus leaving uncovered a crank space of about one-sixth of the circumference, which it was necessary to have in order to provide room for the change in relative position of the shoes due to the angularity of the connecting rods. In the experimental engine the connecting-rod shoes were all given their bearing directly on the crank pin, as heretofore described, being held in contact therewith by means of cone nuts, which were screw-threaded to the crank pin, the taper of the cones permitting adjustment for wear. This method of connecting these parts to the crank pin is the usual plan of connecting three or more connecting rods to one crank pin. So much trouble had been experienced with the water jackets and with minor defects in the experimental engine that no long runs had been possible with it, and consequently no trouble had been experienced because of the small amount of bearing area provided by this method of joining the connecting rods to the crank pin. When, however, the new engine was completed it was found that after working at high power for a few minutes the connecting-rod shoes heated so rapidly that it was impossible to run the engine for more than ten or twelve minutes, the excessive heating of the shoes causing a great diminution in power besides the danger of serious damage if the tests were continued longer. At first this defect seemed almost fatal, as there appeared to be no way of providing sufficient bearing area for the five connecting rods on one crank pin. Happily, however, the writer was able to overcome this defect by an improved design which enables all five connecting rods to operate on the one crank pin, and at the same time provides each with the full amount of bearing area which it would have were it the only connecting rod operating on the crank pin. This arrangement consists essentially of a main connecting rod formed of a steel forging terminating in a sleeve which encircles the crank pin and is provided with a bronze lining for giving a proper bearing surface between the connecting rod and the crank pin, both the steel sleeve and the bronze lining being split, but at right angles to each other, to permit assembling them on the crank pin. This steel sleeve, the upper half of which is formed integral with the main connecting rod is rounded off to a true circle on its exterior circumference, except at the point where the rod joins it. The other four connecting rods terminating in bronze shoes are then caused to bear on the exterior of this sleeve, being held

146

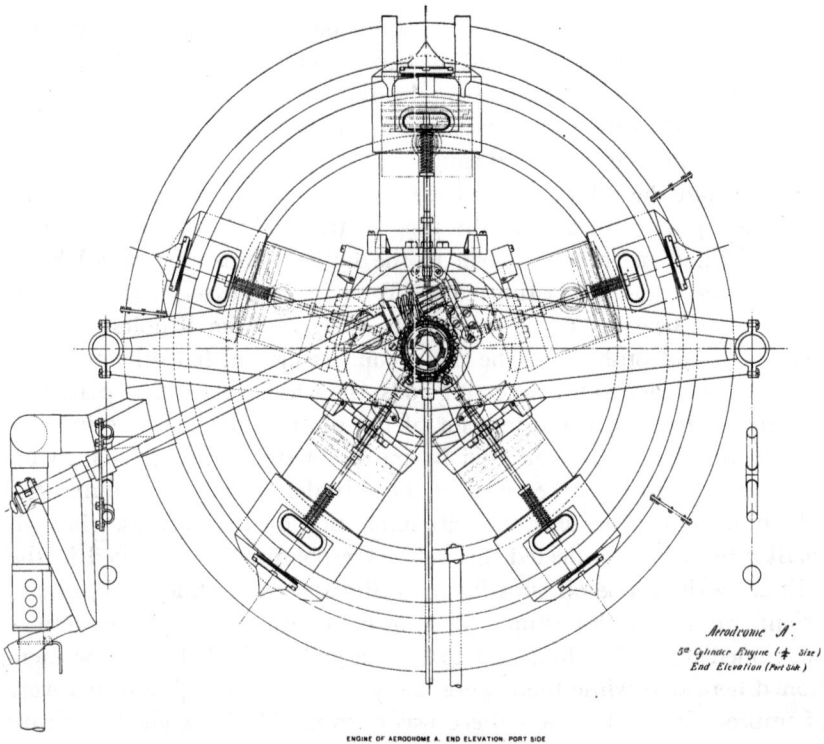

ENGINE OF AERODROME A. END ELEVATION. PORT SIDE

FIGURE 40.—Balzer-Manly engine showing exhaust side. (From "Langley Memoir On Mechanical Flight," Smithsonian photo A19874–A.)

in contact therewith, and permitted to have a sliding motion thereon sufficient to take care of the variation in angularity of the connecting rods, by means of the cone nuts which are screw-threaded to the sleeve and locked thereto by means of the jam nuts, as shown in the drawings. The main connecting rod, of course, acts in the same way as in the ordinary case where each cylinder has its separate crank pin. The other four connecting rods deliver their effort to the crank pin through the sleeve in which the first connecting rod terminates, and they, therefore, do not receive any of the rubbing effect due to the rotation of the crank pin, except that of slipping a very short distance over the circumference of the sleeve during each revolution, the amount of slipping depending on the angularity of the connecting rod. This improved type of bearing was successful from the time of its first trial; and even in later tests in which the engine was run for ten consecutive hours at full power it showed no signs whatever of overheating.

* * * *

147

The lubrication of the main crank-shaft bearing and of the crank pin was effected by means of a small oil cup, fastened to the port bed plate, which fed oil through a hole in the hub of the drum to a circular groove formed in the bronze bushing in the hub. The crankshaft being hollow, a hole was drilled through it in line with the groove in the bushing, and the oil was then led from the interior of the crankshaft through a pipe connected to the plug in the end thereof, and through a hole drilled in the crank arm to the hollow crank pin. Small holes through the crank pin permitted oil to pass to the exterior thereof and thus oil the bearing of the main connecting rod. Small holes through the sleeve and bushing of the main connecting rod fed oil under the shoes of the other four connecting rods, the small holes being placed in oil grooves formed in the interior of the bronze bushing. The lubrication of the pistons was effected by means of small crescent-shaped oil cups fastened to the outer wall of the cylinders, which distributed the oil equidistantly around the circumference of the pistons, through small tubes which projected through corresponding holes drilled in the cylinder wall. These oil cups for the cylinders were, while small, of sufficient size to furnish a supply for approximately one hour, and were so positioned on each cylinder as to have a gravity feed. It may be mentioned here that while there were many parts of the engine which were of unprecedented lightness there was nothing which excelled these oil cups in this respect, as they were made of sheet steel .003 of an inch thick, riveted and soldered up. The crankshaft bearing in the starboard drum was oiled from an oil cup mounted on the outside of the bed plate and connected by a pipe to a hole in the inner wall of the drum, which was connected to the oil grooves in the bronze bushing in the hub of the drum.

The first set of pistons for this engine were similar in design to those shown in the assembled drawings, [not reproduced herein], except that they had side walls and heads which were twice as thick as those shown. These lighter pistons were constructed later, and were just as good as the earlier and heavier ones. It will be noted that the pistons have two deep but thin ribs reinforcing the head. The pistons were slightly tapered from the middle, where they were .005 inch smaller than the cylinder bore, toward the outer end, where they were .0075 inch smaller than the bore. The outer piston ring was .0035 inch narrower than its groove, the second one .003 inch, and the third .0025 inch, and the inner one .002 inch narrower than its groove. The rings were bored one-sixteenth inch off center with the exterior surface, and had one-eighth inch diameter of spring. They were of the lap-joint

148

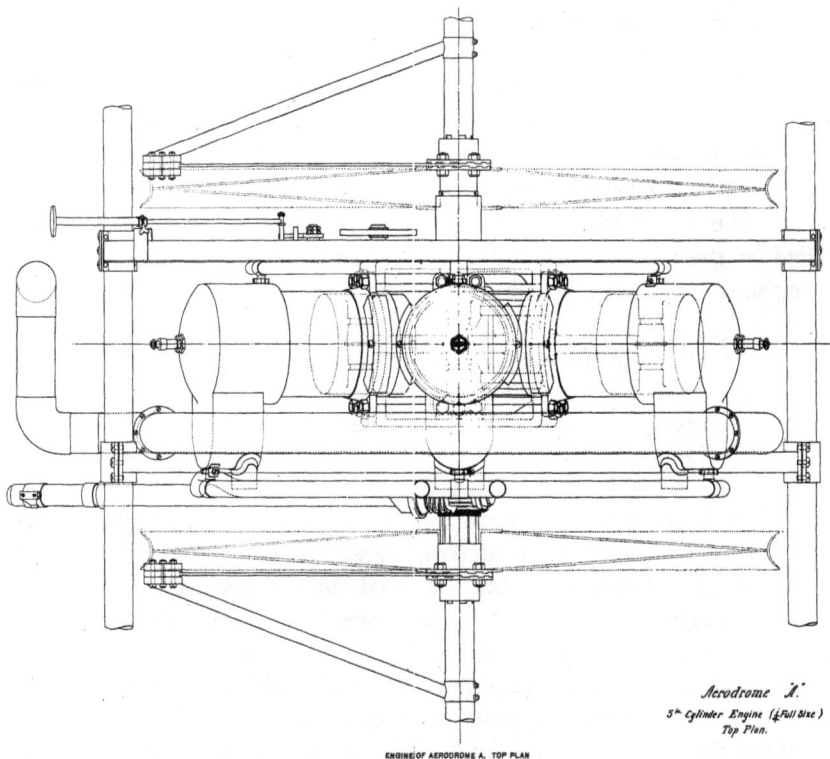

Aerodrome "A."
5ᵗʰ Cylinder Engine (⅓ Full Size)
Top Plan.

ENGINE OF AERODROME A. TOP PLAN

FIGURE 41.—Balzer-Manly engine, top view. (From "Langley Memoir On Mechanical Flight," Smithsonian photo A19874-D.)

type, with the sides of the laps carefully fitted and only one-sixty-fourth-inch clearance at the ends of the laps to allow for thermal expansion. As no grinding facilities were obtainable in Washington, the cylinders were carefully bored smooth and free from taper, and the pistons were worn in to a perfect fit by running them in by a belt for twenty-four hours, with copious oil supply.

The main connecting rod was ⅞ inch diameter and solid, while the other four were of the same diameter but with a ⅝ inch hole in them. The gudgeon pins in the pistons were hollow steel tubes ⅞ inch diameter and case-hardened, and were oiled entirely by the oil thrown off by centrifugal force from the crank-pin bearing, the oil running along the connecting rods and through suitable holes at the heads into oil grooves in the bronze bushings in these heads.

Since on an engine for an aerodrome the best plan for releasing the exhaust gases from the engine is to get rid of them as soon as possible,

149

so long as they are released behind the aviator and do not interfere with his view in the direction of motion, it was decided to have the gases exhaust immediately from the combustion chambers; but in order to prevent their playing on and heating the main bearing of the crankshaft in the port drum the combustion chambers were each provided with a chamber below the exhaust-valve seat, with a side outlet therefrom. The manifold pipe through which the gaseous mixture was supplied to the inlet valves of the engine consisted of a tube bent to a circle and having five branch tubes, each leading to one of the automatic inlet valves, which fitted removable cast-iron seats fastened by a nut in the upper part of each combustion chamber. The very small amount of clearance between the engine and the frame necessitated that this pipe be cut in three places and joined by flanges in order to properly assemble it on the engine when the latter was mounted in the frame. The carbureter, which was placed near the rear of the aviator's car, was connected through suitable pipes to this circular inlet pipe, at a point horizontally in line with the center of the shaft. The auxiliary air valve consisted of a sleeve rotatably mounted on the vertical pipe leading from the carbureter to the manifold, holes in the sleeve being brought to coincide more or less with holes in the vertical pipe, by the operator, when more or less air was required or when he wished to vary the speed of the engine. The cooling water for the jackets of the cylinders was led to them through a circular manifold pipe on the starboard side connected by a vertical pipe with the centrifugal pump situated at the lower point of the lower pyramid of the aerodrome frame. The heated water was led from the jackets through another circular manifold pipe on the port side, through two connections to the radiating tubes at the front and rear, respectively, of the crossframe. These radiating tubes, which were provided with thin radiating ribs soldered to them, finally led the cooled water to the tank situated in the extreme rear of the aviator's car, a suitable pipe from the bottom of this tank being connected to the inlet side of the centrifugal pump. The centrifugal pump was driven by means of a vertical shaft connected to the crankshaft through a set of bevel gears which drove it at three times the speed of the engine. The bearings through which these gears were connected were mounted on the port bed plate, and in order to allow for a certain amount of vibration between the engine and the pump this vertical connecting shaft had a telescoping section connection through suitable splines.

The sparking apparatus comprised, first, a primary sparker similar to the simplest form of such devices which have since come into common use, where a cam driven by the engine co-acts with a pawl on the end of a spring, but in this case, as the sparker was used for all five cylinders, the cam was driven at a speed of two and one-half times that of the engine shaft, thus making and breaking the primary circuit five times in each two revolutions of the engine. Second, a spark coil, the primary terminals of which were connected to the primary sparker and to a set of dry batteries. Third, a secondary distributor consisting of a disc carrying

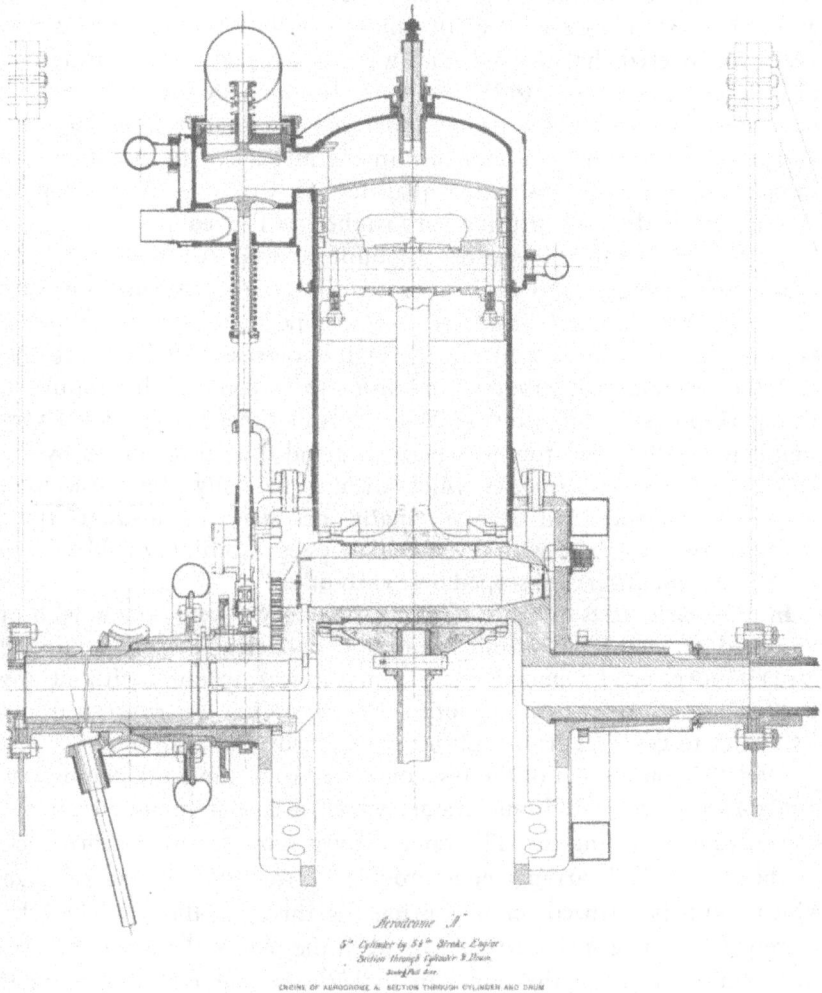

FIGURE 42.—Balzer-Manly engine, cross-section view. (From "Langley Memoir On Mechanical Flight," Smithsonian photo A19874–C.)

151

a contact brush and driven at a speed of one-half that of the engine, this brush being constantly connected through a contact ring to one of the terminals of the high-tension side of the spark coil and running over the face of a five-section commutator, each of the sections of which was connected to a spark plug, the other high-tension terminal of the spark coil being, of course, grounded on the engine frame. This sparking apparatus was first constructed by using blocks of red fibre for insulation. After the engine was completed and was being tested difficulties were met with in the sparking apparatus which at that time appeared inexplicable. After a great deal of annoyance and loss of time it was finally discovered that the red fibre was not as good an insulating medium as it was supposed to be, owing to the zinc oxide used in making it. In damp weather the sparking apparatus absolutely refused to work, and it was found that the moisture in the air caused he zinc oxide in the fibre to nullify its insulating qualities. This trouble, after being located, was cured by substituting hard rubber for the red fibre.

At the time when this engine was built, as well as earlier when the experimental engine was built, it was impossible to procure any wire which had been properly insulated to withstand the high voltages necessary for the connections between the high-tension side of the spark coil and the secondary distributor, and from the secondary distributor to the spark plugs in the cylinders. While at this time this appears a very simple matter, yet the trouble experienced and the delays caused by the lack of such small accessories which are now so easily procurable were very exasperating, and it was finally necessary to insulate these wires by covering them with several thicknesses of ordinary rubber tube of different diameters telescoped over each other.

In the early tests of this new engine, which were made with it mounted on a special testing frame and delivering its power to the water absorption dynamometers, the engine was operated without any flywheels, and, so far as its smoothness of operation was concerned and its ability to generate its maximum power, it did not require any.

After the completion of the tests on the testing frame the engine was assembled in the aerodrome frame, which was first mounted on the floor of the launching car. The car itself was mounted on a short track in the shop, which arrangement provided a smoothly rolling carriage which could be utilized for measuring the thrust of the propellers by merely attaching a spring balance between the rear of the car and a proper holding strap on the track. In the first tests of the engine under these conditions, it was found that while the engine itself did not require any flywheels, yet the lack of them caused trouble with the transmission and propeller shafts, which, while it had never been antici-pated, was easily understood when it was encountered. This difficulty was caused by "reverse torque," which fluctuated from a maximum to a minimum five times during each double revolution of the engine, and which set up fluctuating torsional strains of such magnitude in the transmission and propeller shafts that the shafts themselves became ex-ceedingly hot after a few minutes operation of the engine, and under more prolonged periods of operation these fluctuating torsional strains caused a permanent twisting and bending of the shafts.

* * * * *

Upon calculation it was found that by providing specially light fly-wheels the major portion of this reverse torque could be eliminated for a less increase in weight than would be occasioned by sufficiently in-creasing the thickness of the transmission and propeller shafts to safely stand it.

* * * * *

It will be recalled that in starting up the engine on the quarter-size model, the initial "cranking" necessary with a gasoline engine was ac-complished by having two of the mechanics turn the propellers. While this same plan might have been followed in the case of the large aero-drome, yet it would have involved some danger to the mechanics and would also have left the aviator without any means of restarting the en-gine should it for any reason stop while in the air. Believing it to be very important to provide means for enabling the aviator to restart the engine in case it stopped in the air, the writer devised the starting mechanism shown [See Figures 39 and 40].

* * * * *

This starting mechanism was a success from the first, and the engine was never started up in any other way.

* * * * *

The reason for building the engine with five cylinders instead of some other number, and for arranging them radially on a central drum using only one crank pin may not appear quite obvious. The advan-tages gained by such a construction, however, are very great, and may be briefly summed up as follows:

First, since in a gas engine of the four-cycle type there is only one ex-plosion in each cylinder every two revolutions, and the crankshaft and crank pin therefore are loaded only one-quarter of the time for each

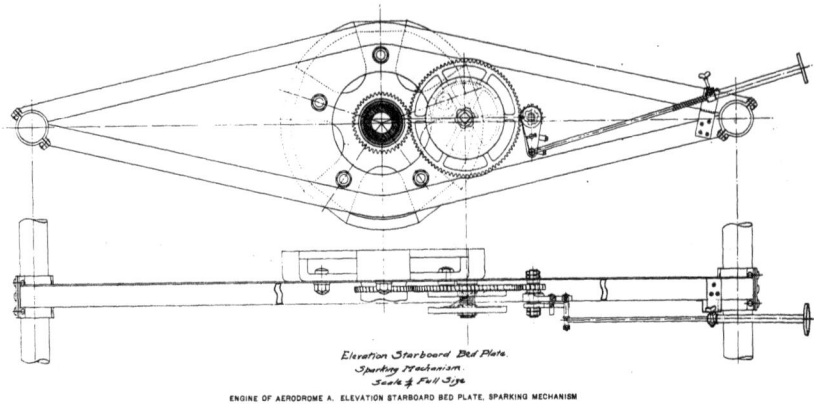

Elevation Starboard Bed Plate.
Sparking Mechanism.
Scale ⅓ Full Size

ENGINE OF AERODROME A. ELEVATION STARBOARD BED PLATE, SPARKING MECHANISM

FIGURE 43.—Balzer-Manly engine, ignition distributing and timing system. (From "Langley Memoir on Mechanical Flight," Smithsonian photo A19874-B.)

cylinder, it is obvious that by having four cylinders arranged radially around a central drum the load on the bearings of a single crankshaft and crank pin may be kept very uniform. However, with four cylinders thus arranged it is impossible to have the cylinders explode and exert their effort on the crank at uniform intervals. With any odd number of cylinders the explosions will occur at equal intervals in the cycle. It is therefore seen that there is a great advantage in smoothness of operation and uniformity of torque of the engine through having an odd number of cylinders instead of an even number.

Second, it is readily apparent that the greater the number of cylinders, provided the number is an odd one, the more uniform the torque will be. There is considerable fluctuation of the torque in each revolution of the engine with five cylinders, but this fluctuation of torque is more easily smoothed out by the use of very light flywheels than by increasing the number of cylinders, and thus adding to the complication of the engine.

Third, the strongest point in favor of the radially arranged cylinders is the reduction in weight and complication which it permits. The crankshaft is reduced to the very minimum, there being only one crank pin with two main bearings which can, without any difficulty whatever, be kept absolutely in line with each other and thus prevent binding and loss of power. Again, the use of a single-throw crank not only reduces the cost and weight of the crank itself, but makes it very much less liable to damage; long crankshafts with several crank pins being

154

frequently twisted by improper explosions in the cylinders. The supporting drum or crank chamber is likewise reduced to the very minimum, both in weight and simplicity, the drums being perfectly symmetrical with no lost space either inside of them or on their exteriors.

* * * * *

The radial arrangement of the cylinders is thus seen to give not only an engine with the smallest number of parts, each of which is as far as possible worked to a uniform amount during each complete revolution of the crankshaft, but it also gives a very compact and readily accessible mechanism with its center of gravity coincident with its center of figure, and with the liability of damage to it, in case of a smash of the vehicle on which it is used, reduced to the minimum from the fact that the greatest weight is located at the strongest part.

Fourth, and of almost as great importance as the reduction in weight which the five-cylinder radial arrangement permits, is its unusual qualities as regards vibration. It is sufficient to call attention to the fact that in an engine having five cylinders arranged radially, all of the reciprocating parts are balanced for all forces of the first, second and third orders. As it is only the reciprocating parts which give any trouble in balancing any engine, the unbalanced rotating parts being readily balanced by placing an equal weight at an equal distance from the center of rotation, and on the opposite side thereof, it is readily seen that the properties of balancing which are inherent in this type of engine are unusual. While this is true as regards the vibration due to moving masses, it is still more impressively true as regards vibration due to reaction arising from the force of the explosions in the engine cylinders, especially when the engine is running slowly and having heavy explosions.

This concludes the excerpts from, "The Langley Memoir on Mechanical Flight."

The engine was completed in December 1901 and was tested in January 1902; however, it did not reach its full horsepower capability until March 1903. Subsequently, under a Prony brake load of 52.4 hp at 950 rpm, it ran continuously for 10 hours during three separate tests. The net dry weight of the engine proper was 124.2 lb. with 20 lb. of cooling water, flywheels, batteries, and accessories, the total weight of the powerplant was 207.5 lb., or 3.96 lb. per hp.[69]

SPECIFICATIONS

Cylinders	— 5 in radial configuration
Cooling	— Water
Carburetion	— Surface type, no float
Ignition	— Battery, induction coil, spark plug (high tension)
Horsepower	— 52.4 at 950 rpm
Bore and stroke	— 5 x 5.5 in.
Displacement	— 540.2 cu. in.
Dimensions	— 37–in. diameter and 19–in. width
Weight	— 207.5 lb. including cooling water
Weight/hp ratio	— 3.96 lb. per hp
Country of manufacture	— U.S.A.

The Balzer-Manly engine was superior to the Wright brothers engine in total horsepower developed (4 times as much), in weight/horsepower ration (4 times lighter), and in reserve power (one-half of total power compared with one-third).

According to the "Langley Memoir on Mechanical Flight,"[70] 28 horsepower was needed to power the aerodrome in its final configuration. This could easily be provided with one cylinder inoperative. The Wright brothers calculated that the "Kitty Hawk Flyer" needed 8 horsepower to fly.[71]

The Balzer-Manly engine was also superior to the Clement engine in total horsepower developed (17 times as much), and in weight/horsepower ratio (2 times lighter). We do not know what Santos Dumont considered the reserve power of his Clement engine to be.

---

[69] This information and the specifications following are from MEYER, op. cit., p. 362.

[70] p. 224.

[71] MARVIN W. McFARLAND, editor, *The Papers of Wilbur and Orville Wright* (New York: McGraw-Hill Book Company, Inc., 1953), vol. 1, p. 313.

Chapter 8

Evaluation of Balzer's and Manly's
Contributions to the Engine

As mentioned in the Prologue, Manly was awarded the Langley Medal posthumously. This presentation was largely due to a statement by Mr. Charles L. Lawrance, President of the Wright Aeronautical Corporation, before the International Civil Aeronautics Conference held in Washington, D.C., 12 to 14 December 1928.[72]

I wish particularly to call your attention to this engine, for if the Wright brothers were geniuses in the science of aerodynamics, as well as in the engineering judgment and good sense which characterized the conduct of their successive experiments, and if Glenn Curtiss was the practical type of engine designer most likely to succeed, Charles Matthews Manly was certainly the outstanding genius of early powerplant design. When we consider that the most popular type of airplane engine of today is almost identical in its general detail and arrangement with the one evolved by Charles Manly in 1902, we are lost in admiration for a man who, with no data at his disposal, no examples of similar art on which to roughly base his design, and no workmen capable of making the more difficult parts of his engine, nevertheless, through the processes of a logical mind, the intelligent application of the science of mathematics, and the use of his surprising mechanical skill, succeeded in constructing an engine developing 52.4 hp for a weight of 125 lb., or a weight of 2.4 lb. per hp.,[73] which stood up under severe tests, once even going through a full power, non-stop run of ten hours.

---

[72] CHARLES L. LAWRANCE, "The Development of the Airplane Engine in the United States," *Mechanical Engineering*, vol 51, no. 3 (March 1929), pp. 186–192.

[73] With 20 pounds of cooling water, flywheels, batteries, and accessories, the total weight of the powerplant was 207.5 pounds, or 3.96 pounds per horsepower.

After giving many details Mr. Lawrance concluded:

Everything had to be specifically made, the ignition system, the carbureter, and even the spark plugs. This engine may indeed be characterized as the first 'modern' aircraft engine in the world, and the fact that it was produced years ahead of any other modern engine, and by an American engineer, should be a matter of pride to all who are interested in the advancement of American aeronautics and the mechanical genius of the American people.

The Langley Medal was awarded for "specially meritorious investigations in connection with the science of aerodromics and its application to aviation." The awarding of the Langley Medal to Manly started a controversy between Balzer and the Smithsonian and involved active correspondence over a two year period. A lot of effort was wasted on both sides in overclaiming, and in trying to prove prior art. Some positive good did result, however, in that the engine label was corrected to reflect Balzer's contributions, and several affidavits were written by mechanics who had served under both Balzer and Manly. These affidavits have been a great help in determining Balzer's and Manly's contributions.

1 June 1931—Stephen M. Balzer in Andover, New Jersey, to Dr. Charles G. Abbot at the Smithsonian Institution. This letter started the controversy.

Last winter it came to my attention that Mr. Charles M. Manly had been signally honored by the Smithsonian Institution for his work in "designing and building" the engine with which Secretary Langley's Aerodrome was powered. It was my privilege for several years to be closely associated with Secretary Langley as well as with Mr. Manly, and it gave me great pleasure to see that Mr. Manly's hard work had been recognized by the Institution he had so ably served.

That pleasure, however, was somewhat dampened since the achievement for which he was especially honored was not his but my own. Furthermore I feel sure that had Mr. Manly been alive he would have seen to it that I received credit for the design of the motor, however much he may have achieved in other lines for the science of engineering.

Although not perhaps of as wide general interest, it appears to me that there is a parallel between the Smithsonian's act in this matter and its actions in the controversy with Orville Wright, since in that quarrel

Professor Langley had no part, so in this question Mr. Manly has no part.[74]

These are the facts, and here are the proofs:

HISTORY The motor wagon on exhibit in the Institution, in the same room with the "Manly engine," was completed by me in 1894. This wagon is equipped with the same type of wood filled carbureter as was used in the Aerodrome. In 1895 I built another motor wagon, similar in all respects but somewhat improved. In 1896 I built still another, but with the cylinders of its engine water cooled. In my preliminary dealing with the Smithsonian Institution preparatory to the signing of the contract, the engine from this wagon was shipped to the Institution, and tested in the presence of Mr. Watkins, Curator, both as a rotary and as a static radial, the crankshaft being provided with a flywheel. The ignition system on this engine was of the make and break type, and it, like its predecessors was a three cylinder. The jump-spark type of ignition, including platinum wire electrode spark plugs was used on other of my rotary and radial engines prior to the signing of the Smithsonian contract. In 1898 I contracted with Secretary Langley "for the Institution" for the design and construction of the engine that was used in the Aerodrome, and later for the design and construction of the smaller engine that is at present on exhibit in the Institution in the quarter size model of the Aerodrome.

PROOF I have a number of letters from both Secretary Langley and Mr. Manly showing not only that I designed and built the motor but showing further that in increasing the horespower to meet the increased requirements of the Aerodrome, owing to its unexpected weight from strengthening the frame, Mr. Manly sought and received my help in carrying out the original and at that time unique work of shrinking the liners in his large size cylinders. We found that the original engine frame and various other parts were strong enough with plenty of factor of safety to take the 5 inch bore, with the same stroke. Finally, the patents for the engine are in my name and were applied for by me before I had the pleasure of meeting either Secretary Langley or Mr. Manly. Even a superficial examination of the "Manly engine" in the Institution and the Balzer engine in the wagon, also in the same room of the Institution, will show a striking likeness between the two. I would be only too glad to furnish you with any further proofs that you may call upon me for.

It has taken me many months to come to the decision that it is due

---

[74] This controversy is summarized by C. G. Abbot, "The 1914 Tests of the Langley 'Aerodrome'," *Smithsonian Miscellaneous Collections*, Vol. 103, no. 8, 1942.

my reputation as an engineer and designer, and at the urgent requests of my friends, to write you, since the two men most concerned, Secretary Langley and Mr. Manly are dead. While work was progressing on the engine, Secretary Langley requested that I keep all information regarding it a confidential trust until the Aerodrome had been successfully flown, at which time he assured me that he would have my part in the project given full publicity. I have faithfully kept this trust, and it is only the fact that the honor for my work has been conferred on another that prompts me to write you.

11 July 1931—Abbot at Smithsonian Institution to Balzer in Andover, New Jersey

Since receiving your letter of June 1, I have been closely engaged in preparing the manuscript of Volume V of the Annals of the Astrophysical Observatory, so that it is only in the last week that I have been able to give attention to the matter of the engine.

I have read all the letters received by the Institution from you and all the letters sent by the Institution to you, as well as many reports, which at that time were confidential, from the Institution to the Board of Ordnance and Fortification, from Manly to Langley and from Langley to Manly, bearing upon the subject. I have also read in full Chapters VIII and X of Manley's "Langley Memoir on Mechanical Flight." [75] I think there can be no question but that, as you claim, the engines which were used in the large and small aerodromes in 1903 resembled in appearance the type of your general design. You will be interested, however, in the quotations, which I append and make a part of this letter, from these formerly confidential sources to which I have referred, and which are enumerated in the following paragraph, as well as in the drawings and description of the final large engine given by Manly in Chapter X above cited: [76]

It seems to me that the accomplishments of Mr. Manly: (a) in passing from a brake horsepower of 8 to one of 20 by modifying the large engine which you contracted for and on which you had spent 18 months; and (b) in achieving reliability and a horsepower of 52 in the new engine made here under his direction which was actually used in the large aerodrome, with a total weight including cooling water and

---

[75] *Smithsonian Contributions to Knowledge,* vol. 27, no. 3, 1911.

[76] Balzer to Langley, 5 December 1898 (page 35); Langley to Manly, 20 June 1900 (page 75); Rathbun to Captain Lewis, 6 September 1900 (page 161); Manly to Langley, 1 January 1901 (page 162); and Report on Progress of Smithsonian Institution to Ordnance Board (page 165).

flywheel of only 207 pounds; and (c) his accomplishment in passing from a horsepower of less than 1 to between 2 and 3 by modifying the small engine of your construction which was used with the quarter-sized model: and this at a time when neither the makers in this country nor in Europe could encourage Dr. Langley to hope for success as regards sufficient lightness and reliability of action for use in the aerodromes; all these achievements entitled Mr. Manly to receive the award which was made by the Institution.

At the same time, I am appreciative of the fact that your relations with Dr. Langley and Mr. Manly were always of the most cordial and helpful sort and that you spent upon your contracts not only your own time and thought but, as Mr. Manly states, $8,000 or $10,000 of your own money beyond that which, according to the contracts, you were paid. I am very ready, therefore, to consider what acknowledgment on the part of the Institution would seem to give you proper credit in the premises. Would it meet your view, for instance, if the Institution should publish a pamphlet quoting your letter of June 1 with such modifications as you might now wish to make, and including quotations from the confidential reports of the Institution by Manly and Langley written at the time, such as I am enclosing? Such a publication might be introduced by a statement from myself acknowledging on behalf of the Institution its appreciation of your efforts in this connection.

Here follow various enclosures mentioned in the above letter which have not already been included in the text; see footnote 76.

6 September 1900—R. Rathbun in Washington, D.C., to Captain L.N. Lewis, Recorder, Board of Ordnance and Fortification, Washington, D.C.

Mr. Powell telephoned me on Tuesday that you were about preparing the annual report of the Board of Ordnance and Fortification, and desired to include in it a brief statement of the progress of the aerodromic work during the year just closed. As Mr. Langley is still abroad and will probably not return before the latter part of October, I have thought it best to give you the following notes, which are merely supplemental to the report of Mr. Langley of October 14, 1899, and which I have obtained from Mr. Manly, leaving it to your discretion how to use them.

Generally speaking, it may be said that the aerodrome is now about ready for its first trial, with the exception of the engine. The wings have been greatly improved since you last visited the work; a full set with duplicates has been entirely completed and is ready for use. The frame of the aerodrome itself, ready for the reception of the engine, is also in a finished state and has been found very satisfactory as regards strength. The steering mechanism, with its duplicate, is also complete and ready for use. The very extensive launching apparatus, built as a superstructure to the house boat was completed this spring and is assembled in its proper position on the house boat. This launching carriage, which immediately supports and carries the aerodrome, is also finished and very satisfactory, while the propellers and the large number of other minor accessories are also ready for use.

The engine, which was being constructed under contract by Mr. Balzer, has failed to fulfill the required conditions, having developed only about two-thirds the power required. A very thorough search both in this country and in Europe for a builder of a suitable engine, has failed to discover one willing to undertake the contract, or, in fact, to offer any assistance whatever. It has therefore become necessary to undertake the construction here and this is now going on under Mr. Manly's supervision. In order to save time and expense, the Balzer engine, the parts of which were admirably constructed, has been brought to Washington and is now being utilized in this work.

Mr. Manly states that he expects to get a preliminary test of the engine under the changed conditions by the close of the present week, but thinks it unsafe to expect immediate success.

During the year the one-quarter size working model of the large aerodrome has been constructed, and it had been hoped that some tests with this would be made before the close of summer, but owing to the failure of the small engine which Mr. Balzer was also building for this, no tests have yet been possible, though everything with the exception of the engine is entirely completed.

If you can find the opportunity, before finally completing your report, to call at the Institution, I feel very certain that you will be able to more readily appreciate the very good progress which has been made during the year.

1 January 1901—Manly to Langley both in Washington, D.C. (in part)

I have the honor to submit for your consideration a report on the condition of the aerodromic work at the close of December, 1900, with a review of the progress which has been made during the past year, and a statement of the work remaining to be done before the large aerodrome will be ready for its field trials.

GREAT AERODROME
Engine

The rotary cylinder gasoline engine which was intended as the first of two similar ones each of which was to be of 12 brake hp and weighing 100 lbs., and which was contracted for by Mr. Balzer on the 12th of December, 1898, to be completed in 10 weeks from that date, was given its first Prony brake test on the 9th of May, 1900, and developed unsteadily for a few minutes, approximately 4 horsepower. After spending 6 weeks from the 6th of May to the 17th of June in New York City at Mr. Balzer's shops in personally looking after the work, though all orders of course still passing through Mr. Balzer's hands, the engine was finally made to develop 8 horsepower steadily, this increase in horsepower however having been accomplished only after a series of the most tedious tests and changes. These changes consisted partly in improving the "wiping contact" sparking arrangement, partly in additions to the combustion chamber to prevent the leakage of compression, also in remodeling and enlarging the rotating inlet sleeve.

There then being very little reason to believe that Mr. Balzer would be successful with this engine, since the past thirteen months had been devoted to a most discouraging series of tests and changes, and there being no engine builders in this country willing to undertake the construction of such a one, and after having under your orders made a brief trip to Europe in June, and there so far as time allowed, made a careful search among the principal builders in England, Germany, France, and Belgium, for one willing to undertake it, I was unable to find anyone who would attempt such a construction.

I may refer in this same connection to the interview you yourself had with Mr. Maxim and also a subsequent one with Comte de Dion, the results of which are given in your letters to me of July 11 and July 30th.[77]

Briefly it may be said that both Mr. Maxim and Comte de Dion were opposed to the rotary form of engine, and that they also agreed that nothing could be done with other forms to procure a suitable engine weighing not more than 4 kilos to the horsepower except after long experiment with an indefinite prospect of success. Mr. Maxim thought that with an engine of the ordinary form, a cylinder 3 inches in diameter with a 6 inch stroke could be made to develop 3 horsepower at a weight of 10 or 12 pounds to the horsepower, and offered you the use of

---

[77] Langley to Manly, 11 July 1900 (page 77); Langley to Manly, 30 July 1900 (page 80). See also Langley memorandum, 10 July 1900 (page 77); and Langley memorandum, 30 July 1900 (page 78).

a workshop and skilled workmen to undertake such a construction; but his engineer, as I understood you, was not so confident. The results which Comte de Dion thought possible are given in detail in your letter to me of July 30th.

I returned from Europe, reaching New York August 13th, and immediately made an inspection of the changes which Mr. Balzer had been making on the engine during my absence. The results of this inspection was that I found that whereas the engine had been developing 8 horsepower when I left it on June 17th, it was now developing only 6 horsepower.

Having previously consulted with you and learned your wishes in case the Balzer engine should finally fail, and believing it to be for the best interest of the work to procure for further experimental purposes the parts of this engine which Mr. Balzer had built, the advantage in these as mere parts being fully worth the contract price of the engine, I accordingly directed Mr. Balzer to ship the engine immediately to Washington. On August 15th I returned to Washington, and as soon as the engine was received, commenced a series of radical changes in it both with respect to the principle and also minor details. The record of these changes and the results which I obtained are contained in my letters to you from August 21st to October 9th.[78] Regarding these changes I may say in brief that using the cylinders, bed-plates, crank and various minor parts of the engine which Mr. Balzer had constructed, but with radical changes both in the principle and in the mechanical details, the engine was gradually perfected. The first preliminary run was made on September 7th and at a speed of 750 rpm the horsepower as shown by the Prony brake varied between 12 and 16, the fluctuations being due to the heating and consequent binding of the brake.

While these changes were in progress you wrote on September 30 briefly stating the fact that Mr. Maxim had offered to put his shop and workmen in England at your disposal, and asking if I would hold myself responsible for producing in the Institution shops an engine suitable for the aerodrome, with the understanding that nothing short of 20 horsepower for a maximum weight of 200 lbs. would answer the purpose. In reply to this inquiry I cabled, "Manly will build engine here in reasonable time."

At this time, September 30th, the 5 original cylinders of the engine were still being used, and the circular form of mounting was still re-

[78] Manly to Langley, 21 August 1900 (page 80) ; Manly to Langley, 11 September 1900 (page 86) ; Manly to Langley, 18 September 1900 (page 87) ; Manly to Langley, 9 October 1900 (page 91) .

tained without revolution. However, many changes had been made both in the principle and in the details and the advance from the 8 horsepower obtained just before I went to Europe to the 20 horsepower which was later reached was mainly due to first,—keeping the cylinders stationary,—second, to improved valve gear, which made all of the cylinders work alike, third, to the invention of an effective secondary sparking arrangement which insured each spark occuring in the proper cylinder at the proper time, and to many other minor changes which in themselves appear small, but on which the success of the engine largely depended.

27 September 1901—Langley's Report on Progress of Aerodromic Work on Account of the Board of Ordnance and Fortification from 1 January 1899 to 1 October 1901

In connection with this present report, I may recall to the Board a preliminary report which was made in October, 1899, and which contained a statement of the progress made in the work between January 1st, 1899 and October 14, 1899.

As the Board is probably aware through a statement of condition of the work on September 6, 1900, which was made during my absence from this country, but which was communicated to the Board through its Recorder, Captain I. N. Lewis, the great delays which have occured in the work and which were not anticipated in the beginning, have been occasioned by the failure of the engine builder with whom I had closed a contract before engaging on this work for the Board, to build an engine of sufficient power and of a weight not prohibitory to the success of the work and that after this failure of the engine builder to fulfill his contract, and also after a most thorough and complete search both in this country and in Europe for a competent builder willing to undertake the construction of a suitable engine, I was forced greatly against my wish to undertake the construction of the engine with the very limited facilities at my disposal in the Institution shops.

The entire frame work adapted for utilizing an engine of the type and dimensions originally contracted for, was completed during the spring of 1900, as was also the special houseboat with its essential superstructure carrying its launching apparatus.

After repeated encouragements from the engine builder who had originally contracted for the engine, and a final failure in June, 1900, to fulfill the contract, the search both in this country and in Europe mentioned above for a competent engine builder was instituted, and upon the failure of this search, in August 1900 some of the materials

165

from the original contractor were purchased and made use of in the experiments which were immediately begun in the Institution shops toward the building of an engine suitable for use in the already completed frame. Utilizing some of the parts of this condemned engine, an engine was constructed which on repeated tests proved itself capable of developing horsepower for weight within the limits essential to the success of the work, but unfortunately of not quite large enough size to furnish the full power which I deemed essential to have at the disposal of the aeronaut at the first trials in free flight and until the aeronaut had gained some practice in the manipulation of the machine.

A new larger engine capable of furnishing the full power necessary for the first trials in free flight was begun in the early part of the present year, but unfortunately owing to the serious delay of several months in obtaining the very special materials necessary for the engine, and to other unavoidable delays which have since occurred in the course of construction, this new and larger engine is not yet quite complete, though it is rapidly nearing completion, and will unless some serious accident or delay occur, be ready for a trial during the present month of October, as will also its necessary accessories adapted to its use in the already completed frame.

Every precaution which it has been possible to foresee has been taken to insure a very early trial in free flight upon the completion of the engine, and unless serious delays should occur, which are not expected, but which are always possible in such light constructions, upon the introduction of the high-powered engine in its frame, there appears at present good reason to expect to be able to make the first trial in free flight before the close of the present year.

If the Board should favor me by a visit to inspect the progress of the work, I think that a much more intelligent idea may be formed of its present condition and of the work remaining before the first experiment in free flight is made.

Several months and several letters later the controversy was aired in the press as follows:

25 October 1931—*The New York Times*

LANGLEY AIRPLANE IN NEW DISPUTE

Friends of S. M. Balzer Say He, Not C. M. Manly Invented the Engine.

SCORE NATIONAL MUSEUM

Smithsonian Institution Faces a Controversy Similar to That Which It Had With Orville Wright.

166

The Smithsonian Institution, which several years ago was a party to a lively controversy with Orville Wright over whether the "Langley Aerodrome" was entitled to be called the first man-carrying, heavier-than-air flying machine, is likely to become involved in a related dispute. Mr. Wright, after forcing the museum to change the legend on the cards on the Langley machine, sent his historic airplane, the first ever to fly with a pilot, to the Kensington Museum in Great Britain, where it appears likely to stay instead of in the Smithsonian.

Curiously enough, the Langley Aerodrome, which crashed when Charles M. Manly attempted to fly over the Potomac River, is directly concerned now. Evidence is being gathered to dispute the long-standing claim that Manly designed and built the "Manly-engine," a remarkable power plant in which features in use in aircraft engines today were incorporated and which developed more than fifty horsepower when it was installed in Langley's flying machine.

Friends Press Balzer's Claim.—Friends of Stephen M. Balzer, head of the Balzer Engineering Company of Andover, N. J., and formerly the Balzer Motor Company of New York, have come forward and are pressing vigorously the claim that Balzer, not Manly, designed and built the original engine for which Manly posthumously received the Langley Medal a year ago.

Mr. Balzer himself, however, was reluctant yesterday to talk about the matter. He admitted that with the help of John McK. Ballou, an aeronautical engineer now working on the Merrill safety plane, and others, among them his former employees and his former patent lawyer, he is gathering evidence to prove that he and not Manly designed and built the famous engine, and that even though Manly did rebuild it in the shops of the Smithsonian Institution with larger cylinders, Balzer's mechanics, designs, gauges and jigs were sent to Washington from New York to help in the work.

The five-cylinder radial engine now stands in a glass case beneath the aerodrome in the National Museum, and the last line on the card describing the exhibit reads:

"Built in the shops of the Smithsonian Institution by Charles M. Manly, under the direction of S. P. Langley."

Nearby is an ancient motor vehicle—the first, it is said, ever to run on the streets of New York. It was built by Balzer in 1894 and donated to the Smithsonian at a later date.

It is a development of the engine in this automobile which is now called the Manly engine and which was used in the attempt to fly the Aerodrome. In recalling the history of those early days of the internal combustion engine Mr. Balzer says that he experimented from 1894 until 1898. He could find nothing suitable for spark plugs so he hit upon the idea of employing a maker of false teeth to cast porcelain cores for his platinum wire electrodes. In 1896 he applied for patents on his engines and automobiles which were issued finally in 1903. Long before he was asked by the Smithsonian to build an engine for a flying machine he devised a carburetor that worked successfully as testified by Manly in his memoirs which consisted of a sheet metal shell filled with small pieces of porous wood saturated with gasoline. The supply was kept ample by a feeding valve and the engine sucking air through this shell obtained the mixture necessary for combustion.

For years some of us have been trying to get Mr. Balzer to seek to establish the fact that it was his engine in all its essentials and not Manly's that stands in the Smithsonian today, Mr. Ballou said yesterday; but he said that Professor Langley asked him to say nothing about his work and after Langley's death he felt that the promise still was sacred. It was not until Mr. Manly died and in spite of patent records which can be seen in the bureau today, and after the Smithsonian awarded the Langley medal to Mr. Manly's son for his father's achievements that we persuaded Balzer to let us go ahead and try to establish the facts. In his chapter in the Langley memoirs concerning the engine, Manly did not mention Balzer except as "a builder" whose engine failed, resulting in the transfer of the whole project to Washington. Nowhere does he mention that in rebuilding the engine he sought Balzer's help, used his measurements and jigs, utilized his methods for shrinking on the new cylinders and even had the aid of Balzer's own mechanics in rebuilding the motor.

As in the Wright controversy so in this case, Ballou said, the Smithsonian has not shown any enthusiasm toward correcting their error nor in righting an injury inflicted on a worthy person. Fortunately both Mr. Balzer's automobile and his engine are at present in the National Museum of the Smithsonian Institution and cannot therefore be sent to a British museum as in the case of the original Wright brothers' machine.

Balzer is today strong and active. He works daily in his laboratory, despite his 70 years. He is still confident that if a man with some knowledge of the air had been chosen to fly the ill-fated Langley machine instead of an engineer it might have been the first to fly.

ORIGINAL PLANS FOR MOTOR

In discussing his own work on the engine Mr. Balzer said that it gave them a lot of trouble. Originally it was the plan to build two twelve horsepower engines, but with the increased weight necessary it was decided that one motor which would develop twenty-four horsepower should be sought. While work was progressing on the engine Mr. Balzer was called upon by Professor Langley and Manly to fabricate various other parts of the flying machine, including the main frame supports of the engine, which had at first been built in the shops of the Institution, but, owing to faulty design and construction, had failed, according to Ballou.

In connection with the carbureter which is now on the engine, Mr. Balzer's friends say that credit should be given to him.

When the engine was delivered to the Smithsonian, according to Ballou, it was equipped with a carbureter, if not the one on exhibit, it was certainly a copy of it in every detail, yet the card on it makes no mention of Balzer as its inventor.

The card reads:

"Carbureter of Manly Engine—This is the surface type carbureter consisting of a tank filled with porous wood. . . . This type of Carbureter was selected by Manly after tests of many other types. It kept the engine running even after the Aerodrome turned over on its back."

Nowhere in Manly's writing is Balzer mentioned by name. The motor, according to Manly, failed even after changes, to develop more than four horsepower continuously, so he decided to give up working further on the motor and seek another one elsewhere. He went to Europe but could not find a motor or a motor manufacturer who would build an engine for the Institution so he returned to New York and the "engine builder" again. Here, according to his chapter in the Langley memoirs, Manly found no progress so he promptly condemned the engine and a smaller motor Balzer was building for a model. Manly says that he took the parts of the two engines to Washington as it was hoped that some of the parts of the engines might prove of use in experimental work.

It is the contention of Balzer's friends that instead of using a few parts in experimental work the so-called new engine was built up entirely of these parts or parts modeled exactly on them and for these reasons alone they believe Balzer instead of Manly should be recognized as the designer and creator of the Manly engine.[79]

[79] On 4 April 1932, Dr. Abbot, Secretary of the Institution, took a constructive step by asking one of the six mechanics who had worked for Balzer and Manly to evaluate their contributions to the engine project.

Mr. Stephen Balzer and his friends feel aggrieved by the award recently made to Charles M. Manly, posthumously, by the Smithsonian
Institution of the Langley Gold Medal for Aerodromics. This award
was made largely on account of the high praise given Manly in an international address by Mr. Charles Lawrence, then President of the
Wright Corporation.

Mr. Balzer claims as his achievement the building of the large engine, and desires the Smithsonian to publish the statement I enclose as
a measure of justice to him. Of course the Institution intends to be
strictly just in the matter, and I realize that from your close connection
with the work you know all the circumstances well enough to check Mr.
Balzer's claims.

I am therefore venturing to ask you, who were Manly's associate during many years, for the sake of securing exact justice to his memory, to
carefully consider all the statements of Mr. Balzer's memorandum, and
comment on all that seem to you inexact. For instance he gives the impression that you and Newham and Hewitt were given by him to
Manly as an act of grace and assistance on Balzer's part. Hewitt, however, has told me that he had left Balzer, was working in Connecticut,
and applied to Manly for a job. Possibly you and Newham may have
found Balzer slow pay and preferred to come to Manly on your own
motion.

But the really grave question is whether Balzer is deserving so much
and Manly so little credit for the large engine as Balzer claims in the
latter part of his memorandum. To this I hope you will give particular
attention and make careful comments. I shall understand that wher-
ever you make no comment you accept the statement of the memorandum.

I feel that, recalling your long association with Manly, you will be
willing to perform this service now that he is dead, but I shall be glad
to give you an honorarium of $50 from the Institution to reimburse
you for the time you will have to give if you will kindly assist me as I
have indicated. I am sending a copy of the Manly Memoir in case you
should need to refresh your recollection, and you will please return it
when finished.

*21 April 1932—MacDonald in Milton, Massachusetts, to Abbot in
Washington, D.C.*

I am extremely sorry to keep you waiting so long for this statement of my experience while at the Smithsonian Institution and particularly while working on the Balzer-Manly motors.

Regarding Mr. Stephen Balzer and his friends feeling aggrieved by the recent award to Charles M. Manly, I do not know of any reason why they should feel grieved. In my opinion they are not entitled to any consideration.

Concerning Mr. Manly's associates during the many years I was with him, I can say that I saw very few of them as I don't think there were many. One was Dr. Stratton, who is now dead, and another was William McKay Smith, who has been in charge of the switchboard department of the Western Electric Company on West Street, New York City. I should think that Mr. Smith could give you quite a good deal of information as he had charge of Mr. Manly's laboratory while Mr. Manly was in Buffalo with the Curtiss Company.

In regards to Mr. Balzer giving the impression that he gave us to Mr. Manly, it came about this way:—

Mr. Manly came to us and asked us if we would go down to Washington and work for him at the Smithsonian Institution. Mr. Balzer was willing for us to go inasmuch as he had no more work for us.

In making his engine Mr. Manly had to use some of Mr. Balzer's ideas but he used so few of them that they only have a minor importance. For example, the five cylinder radial disposition about the crank.

I was looking at a three cylinder radial steam engine today that was made 45 years ago with the same crank mounting and exactly the same design as the Balzer crank.[80]

You will see by the new parts as shown in my report that there were only about three old parts used in making the new engine.

You can judge for yourself how much credit is due to Mr. Balzer but my firm belief is that Mr. Manly is deserving of every bit of reward which has been given to him.

RE:—STEPHEN M. BALZER CLAIMS & ACHIEVEMENTS

While I was working at the Balzer shop in New York I saw the automobile and engine that is now in the United States National Museum in Washington, D.C., but I have never seen it running. However, I think it was nearly as good as the last one he made. I saw it and it acted the same as the one he made for the Smithsonian Institution.

In regards to the Gnome, the LeRhone and the Crossley motors, their mechanism is altogether different from the Balzer motor. They have a

---

[80] MacDonald wrote Abbot on 19 May 1932 to say that this steam engine was actually only 34 years old.

closed in crank chamber and take the gas in through the crank chamber and up through the piston head.

The carbureter used on the 52 hp engine was entirely different from the carbureter used on the original Balzer motor as is fully explained on pages 224 and 225 of the Langley "Memoir on Mechanical Flight."

Water Jackets on Cylinders

I can say that I never saw any drawings or any letters from Mr. Balzer where he made any mention of water jacketing the cylinders. That was all planned after the cylinders were held stationary by Mr. Manly. At the first test after holding the cylinders stationary the engine came right up to speed but got terribly hot. We then put a large fan blowing the hot air off. That made a good showing. Then, the next thing was to wet cloths. We kept running cold water on each cylinder.

By this method the first brake test was made. After making several brake tests Mr. Manly decided to stop and put water jackets on the cylinders.

I can't see how Mr. Balzer can make any claim on the water jackets because the engine was made into a stationary cylinder and is no longer a rotary engine.

Ignition

The platinum pointed spark plugs were redesigned by Mr. Manly from one spark plug that came with the Comte de Dion small engine which Professor Langley sent over from France. Comte de Dion single jump spark coil was used on all tests.

Timing Gears and Distributor Advance and Retard Mechanism

The Comte de Dion timing gears and distributor advance and retard mechanism were redesigned by Mr. Manly and made at the Smithsonian Institution.

Utilizing Flywheel and Crankshaft

I saw it and it was nothing more than a friction disc. If you moved out of center one way the car would go ahead. If you moved the other way the car went backwards.

Building the New Engine

When Mr. Manly was building the new engine I don't think he asked help from anyone, and as far as Mr. Balzer having anything to do with it I can't see that he did. Mr. Manly got some tools from Mr. Balzer but I don't think we used them because the small tools would not work on the large motor. Mr. Balzer was never at the Smithsonian Institution in my time. Of course he would have been glad to help out if he had been asked to but there was never a time when we were in trouble. The work always went right along.

NEW PARTS MADE AND REDESIGNED ON MANLY ENGINE

1. Five new cylinders.
   Five inch bore with large valve chambers, cylinders and valve chambers water jacketed with $1/32$ bright metal sheet steel.
2. Five new large intake valves also five new valve cages.
3. Five new exhaust valves.
4. Five new pistons of special design.
5. Five spark plugs designed and made at the Smithsonian Institution, designed by Manly. First five made by R. S. Newham.
6. Circular intake manifold fitting over five intake valves and fastened air tight by flange nuts.
7. Water jacket fittings—two circular manifolds fitted to cylinders with flange nuts.
8. One new crankshaft hammer forged of Krupp steel EF 60.0.
9. One exhaust valve timing cam and timing gear mechanism.
10. One supporting bed plate drum.
11. One worm gear and one worm for motor starting crank.
12. One water pump driving gear and one shaft and pinion.
13. Two flange couplings for crankshaft.
14. Engine supporting bed plate square tubing on sides.
15. Ignition system distributor and timing gears and advance and retard control
16. Two special design flywheels.
17. Two crank pin balancing arms.
18. Crank pin lubricating system.
19. Valve springs.
20. Five punch rods for exhaust valves.
21. Studs and screws.
22. Four connecting rods wrist pin type.
23. Four connecting rod shoes special metal.
24. Two shoe retaining cones.
25. Two jam nuts.
26. One special connecting rod with a full bearing at all angles.

BALZER—"SLIPPER TYPE CRANK AND CONNECTING ROD BEARINGS, PERMITTING ALL FIVE CONNECTING ROD AXES TO LIE IN THE SAME PLANE WHILE OPERATING A SINGLE THROW CRANK."

Slipper type connecting rods will not work having five connecting rod shoes fastened directly to the crank. In the first place you can't oil

173

the connecting rod shoes because there will be much more oil coming out between the shoes than the shoes are getting. I saw the old Balzer motor crankshaft getting so hot that the sparks were flying from it. That was after the cylinders were water jacketted on the long tests. We used to squirt oil from the outside on to the crank but it would come off faster than it went on to the crank pin. The connecting rod shoes have no bearing—about $3\frac{1}{2}$ square inches to start with and when the pressure comes on I doubt if there is $2\frac{1}{2}$ square inches. When the pressure came down on the center of the shoe the ends had a tendency to come up. You can readily see that $2\frac{1}{2}$ inch bearing surface is nothing for a five inch piston having seventy-five to eighty pounds compression to the square inch.

It was thought that by using some different kind of metal in the connecting rod shoes this might remedy the trouble so a new crankshaft was made in the same way. You can see the threads on the crank pin where the cone bearings were screwed on the crank pin.

The engine was finished, assembled, and set up in the testing stand and all adjustments made. The engine started right off and ran like a clock so it was decided to run lightly and let everything wear in. In the meantime we got the dynamometers set and lined up for the brake tests. The dynamometers were coupled up. We started up the engine and ran with part load for about $\frac{1}{2}$ hour. Stopped and found the crank pin hot but not cutting. Cooled off and started again, running with a little more load for about the same length of time. Stopped and found it was still hotter. The next test was more load and longer run until the smoke was coming off the crank pin. Stopped and found the pin starting to cut. The test was stopped and it was decided to try Parson's White Bronze in the connecting rod shoes. Had a pattern made and finished up a set of shoes. Tried them out and found a little improvement but nothing like what was wanted. Just the minute the load was put on it started to heat up and the heavier the load the worse it got. That was when everything looked like complete failure. No bearing surface and no way to oil. What could be done.

After a lot of deep thinking Mr. Manly struck on #1 connecting rod. Would it work? It was made up and tried out and it worked! It not only oiled the crank pin but it also gave the other four connecting rods a full bearing. By #1 connecting rod having a full complete bearing around the crank pin the oil was trapped and wasn't thrown off. The other four connecting rods were mounted around the outside #1 connecting rod and needed very little oil.

This achievement was the key of success for the Manly engine. Take

174

the Manly connecting rods out and put the old ones in and you have complete failure. The engine will burn up in one hour's run—that is with a load.

10 September 1932—C. G. Abbot in Washington, D.C., to Mr. Lloyd N. Scott, 535 Fifth Avenue, New York City

Your letter of August 26 reaches me after my return from New England where I had a very fine view of the eclipse and also visited my relatives.

Mr. Edgar Moore asked me to recommend someone competent to advise him in his legal matters and I could think of no one so likely to be satisfactory as yourself.

The Balzer matter was referred to Basil Manly. He took it up with his brother Prof. John Manly and we received on August 31 a letter, a copy of which I enclose. This letter makes it look as if whatever we might do for Balzer would merely get us into hot water with Manly. Would you advise a conference with Manly to see whether we may get by with the proposed sop to Balzer without objections on the part of the Manly's?

P.S. Do you really think that, in view of Mac Donald's statement, Balzer can do us any harm if we should now inform him that in view of our researches we find the record sufficiently correct and then sit tight?

1 June 1933—Ballou in Andover, New Jersey, to Scott in New York City

Enclosed you will find blue printed copies of three affidavits, in duplicate, one from Mr. Balzer's bookkeeper and secretary at the time of the building of the "Manly Engine," and other two from mechanics who worked first for Mr. Balzer and later for Mr. Manly on the engine. You have also a letter from Mr. George D. Mac Donald, intended, evidently at the request of Mr. Basil Manly, to discredit Mr. Balzer, but definitely substantiating my claims for Mr. Balzer instead. I have a very similar letter from him. You have seen most of the pertinent correspondence in the case, wherein Mr. Charles M. Manly discredits himself by expressing a gross ignorance of the simplest ideas in elementary physics; and again wherein he is requesting advice from Balzer; and still further wherein he is requesting tools and other equipment for the reconstruction of the engine.

I am here with Mr. Balzer for a couple of days while enroute for California. I have discussed the controversy with him again in the light of the three new pieces of evidence, namely, these affidavits, and he is unwilling to submit the matter to settlement, as you suggested, by a committee to be chosen. It is perfectly clear now, that the engine on exhibition in the Smithsonian *IS* the Balzer engine, reconstructed by Manly. You now know the facts, and in fairness to your client as well as to Mr. Balzer, your true duty in representing your client is to find a graceful means of relabelling the engines and publishing the facts. We will not try to dictate the title, but suggest that THE BALZER ENGINE RECONSTRUCTED BY MANLY, or THE ENGINE USED IN THE LANGLEY AERODROME BUILT IN NEW YORK CITY BY STEPHEN M. BALZER UNDER HIS UNITED STATES PATENTS AND RECONSTRUCTED BY CHARLES M. MANLY IN THE SHOP OF THE SMITHSONIAN INSTITUTION, or THE BALZER–MANLY ENGINE, would be truthful and entirely satisfactory to us.

Just because a fraudulent label has been posted on the engine and a medal awarded, perhaps inadvertently, is no reason for those who now know the truth to perpetuate the fraud. Last Fall, you wrote me suggesting that we submit our proofs, altho we had already furnished more than sufficient evidence to establish the facts, including the patent copies. You have now in your hands unrefutable proofs from the pens of an antagonistic witness, a favorable witness, and two impartial but fair minded witnessess, in addition to the letters, pictures (in the files of the Institution) contracts, and verbal opinions.

Please do not make it incumbent upon us to take other steps to rectify this false history. Your efforts at this time can avert much expense to your client and ourselves, and can prevent the publication of much truthful but disagreeable matter against Mr. Charles M. Manly that would certainly come to light if we were forced to go elsewhere for justice and fair play.

14 March 1932—Affidavit sworn by Berthold D. Willenbrock before George H. Hill, Notary Public, New York City

I am a citizen of the United States having a place of business located at 100 East 86th Street, in the City, County and State of New York. I was employed by Mr. Stephen M. Balzer under the title of bookkeeper from September, 1899 until September 1900. My duties in the Balzer shops comprised keeping all of the accounts and records, handling all the correspondence and acting as secretary to Mr. Balzer, determining in the shops the time that the various men devoted to the various jobs in progress, preparing the payroll, receiving the incoming money and disbursing the money to cover accounts payable and the payroll to the men. During said time period of my employ in the Balzer shops in New York City I was in intimate contact with and familiar with all of the work being executed therein, including a large radial gasoline engine and a small radial gasoline engine for the Smithsonian Institution, and with all of the business transactions pertaining to the work of the Balzer shops.

I have read Chapter VIII of the Langley Memoir on Mechanical Flight, and find it to be a combination of statements of facts, of shrewdly stated half-truths, and of direct falsehoods, all carefully arranged with the evident intention of throwing discredit on Mr. Balzer, and leading the reader of said chapter to the false conclusion that Mr. Charles M. Manly and not Mr. Stephen M. Balzer was the originator and constructor of the engine used in Professor Langley's full scale experiments on Mechanical Flight.

Referring to the second paragraph on Page 218 of said Chapter VIII, the statement: "After remaining in New York for several weeks, during which time many changes were made in the engine, he finally got it to the point where it would develop four horsepower continuously; but it seemed impossible to get any better results without an indefinite amount of experiment, it was decided that all hope of making this engine an immediate success would have to be abandoned" is entirely misleading and false. I was present at the Balzer shops every working day from May 6, 1900 until July 1, 1900 and I know that Mr. Manly was not in the Balzer shops for more than two consecutive days separated by an interval of at least two weeks. I do not know where he was, but I do know that he was not at the Balzer shops during the remainder of this time. The engine was developing eight horsepower continuously instead of four.

Referring to the first paragraph on Page 219,—Mr. Manly did not go to Europe about the middle of June, 1900. He was present at a conference in the Balzer shops with Mr. Balzer on June 26, 1900.

Referring to the third paragraph on Page 219,—Mr. Manly did not condemn either the large or the small engine. He accepted both, altho the small one was not complete, and in consideration of its being incomplete Mr. Balzer allowed $100.00 on it, accepting $700 instead of the agreed $800 for it, with the understanding that Messrs. Newham and MacDonald would complete it in the shops of the Smithsonian Institution. These gentlemen were skilled mechanics who had been up to this time in the employ of Mr. Balzer and had become expert in executing the work on the Balzer engines. The statement that Mr. Balzer had practically bankrupted himself in his attempts to build these two engines and had spent $8,000 or $10,000 in actual wages over and above the contract prices, constitutes a direct falsehood. He did not spend any

177

considerable sum over and above the contract prices and the work on these two engines was only a small part of the total work in the Balzer shops.

The first paragraph of Page 220 is a combination of direct falsehoods and shrewd half truths. Preparatory to the acceptance of the two Balzer engines by Mr. Manly, Messrs. Balzer and Manly held a conference at which I was present wherein Mr. Balzer agreed to let his two most skilled mechanics be taken over by the Smithsonian Institution to continue work on the small engine and to make certain alterations in the large engine that Mr. Balzer laid out in detail. These alterations included the substitution of a jump-spark ignition system for the primary electric ignition system at that time on the engine. This jump-spark system was similar to the system used at that time on the Balzer automobile engine, and employed a single buzzing spark coil and a single set of electric batteries with a distributor to lead the spark to the proper cylinder at the proper time. Spark plugs were used in the cylinders. Mr. Balzer showed Mr. Manly one of the Balzer engines embodying this ignition system, and gave him detailed instructions as to its working and construction. These improvements or alterations included also water jackets for the cylinders, brazed up out of sheet steel, to simulate the water jackets cast in the heads of the Balzer automobile engines.

The last two sentences of Page 224 and all of Page 225 of said Chapter VIII is a fairly accurate description of the carbureter that was delivered in August 1900 as part of the equipment of the Balzer engine for use in the Langley Aerodrome from the Balzer shops in New York. I distinctly remember having myself obtained the Tupelo wood and brought it to the Balzer shops for the making there of this carbureter.

I have been in Washington and have seen an engine in a glass case in the National Museum of the Smithsonian Institution that was designated as the Manly engine. I can identify this engine as the Balzer engine, reconstructed with larger cylinders and embodying the improvements suggested by Mr. Balzer to Mr. Manly in August 1900 as hereinbefore described.

I was present at various conferences between Messrs. Balzer and Manly at the Balzer shops, between September 1899 and August 1900. On various occasions at these conferences I was astonished at Mr. Manly's display of ignorance not only of gasoline engines, but of shop practice in general and of even elementary physical science. I have read a letter from Mr. Manly to Mr. Balzer dated September 28, 1900 and find the misconception by Mr. Manly of the simple laws of nature as expressed in said conferences.

178

The aforesaid engine that I saw in Washington retains the following features from the Balzer engine from which it was reconstructed:—

(1) 5 cylinder radial disposition.
(2) Cylinder mounting of two rings that carry also the main bearings.
(3) Steel cylinders shrunk over cast iron liners.
(4) Slipper type connecting rod bearings on a single throw crank.
(5) Hollow crankshaft.
(6) Elongated diamond shape steel tubing engine bearers with sheet steel web brazed to the tubes.
(7) Four cycle timed 1—3—5—2—4.
(8) A two lobed cam for operating the valves.
(9) Tupelo wood filled carbureter.

22 May 1933—Affidavit sworn by Fred Hewitt before Robert T. High-field, Notary Public, Washington, D.C.

I am a citizen of the United States residing in Washington, District of Columbia, where I am editor and manager of the Machinists Journal.[81] I was formerly a resident of New York City where I was graduated from the Technical School of Cooper Union, and where I was working as an expert mechanic. In March of 1900 my friend Richard S. New-ham informed me that he was being released from employment in New York City to enter the employ of the Smithsonian Institution in Washington, and that there would be a vacancy for a competent mechanic. I therefore replaced Mr. Newham in the shop of Mr. Stephen M. Balzer in March, 1900 in the section of New York known as Mott Haven.

While in the employ of said Balzer, I was at times detailed to work on a radial five cylinder gasoline engine that said Balzer had invented and patented and was building on contract for Professor Langley's Aerodrome. I remember that I considered this the most remarkable invention in the way of engines that I had ever seen. While engaged in working on said engine, I became thoroughly familiar with its construction and with the unique features that characterized it. I also became familiar with a small scale replica of said engine, that said Balzer was constructing on contract to the Smithsonian Institution.

About the middle of August, 1900 Mr. Manly of the Smithsonian Institution came to New York and accepted delivery on both engines, altho the smaller one still lacked cooling fins on the cylinders, and the full size one had tested somewhat short of its guaranteed power output.

---

[81] *Machinists Monthly Journal,* was the official organ of the International Association of Machinists, Washington, D. C.

I remained in the employ of the Balzer shop until November, 1900 when I went to work in Norwalk, Connecticut. In January, 1901 I accepted an offer of employment from Mr. Manly in the shop of the said Institution in Washington, and went to work there, where I remained until January, 1904.

Upon my assuming my duties as an expert mechanic in said shop in Washington, I was detailed to construct various parts for the engine that was used in the Langley Aerodrome, and which is at present on exhibit in the National Museum of the Smithsonian Institution, designated as the Manly engine. This engine is a reconstruction of the large Balzer engine hereinbefore referred to, but with larger cylinders substituted for the original ones, with the cylinders held stationary, whereas in the original engine they revolved and the crankshaft was stationary, and with a De Dion design of electric ignition substituted for the make and break electric ignition supplied by Balzer. I constructed new pistons and rings, as the enlarged bore required them, altho the stroke was not changed, and these new pistons were lighter in weight than the original pistons. I also constructed the new combustion chambers for the larger cylinders. The nucleus of this new engine was the two side rings and the knee brackets with the main bearings, the front engine bearer, the cam and timing gear assembly and the valve lifter guides from the original Balzer engine. Mr. Manly secured the drilling jig from Mr. Balzer wherewith to drill the flanges on the new cylinders, to assure their fitting the original Balzer main frame described above. The new, larger cylinders were constructed according to Balzer's method as used on the original cylinders, namely, shrinking the steel tubing cylinders over cast iron liners, and boring in the assembly. The method of construction enabled us to gain sufficient strength, with remarkable lightness as well as excellent resistance to wear, for which the engine is famous. The combustion chambers were brazed to the steel cylinders, and brazed-up water jackets were secured to the cylinders and combustion chambers for cooling. The Balzer construction of the crank pin bearing was improved by using a master rod with a bronze crankpin bushing, upon which the other four connecting rod segments bore, and about which they were retained by end rings similar to Balzer's end rings.

I distinctly recollect how, when it was decided to braze cooling fins on the cylinders of the small replica of the Balzer engine in the shop in Washington, Professor Langley remarked that it seemed a shame to spoil the excellent appearance of the finish by heating them. This small engine, with slight modification was used successfully for flights of a small model of the man-carrying sized Aerodrome. This model, with the modified Balzer engine is on exhibit in the National museum of the Smithsonian Institution.

The Balzer engine, as originally built in New York was equipped with a carbureter comprising a sheet metal envelope containing Tupelo wood fragments into which gasoline was fed. After considerable work had been done at the shop of the Smithsonian Institution in an endeavor to find a substitute for this carbureter, which led Mr. Manly to the conclusion that nothing else was as satisfactory, a larger copy was constructed which was used with the engine in the Aerodrome.

I always had and still have the highest regard for Mr. Manly and for his ability as an engineer as well as for his moral courage that led him to persist in the development of the flying machine in the face of heartbreaking ridicule, and for his physical courage, that led him to risk his life in his attempt to pilot it.

In my estimation, the Manly engine is an enlarged reconstruction of the Balzer engine, and it is reasonable to assume that Manly would never have thought of using a radial engine had he not had Balzer's patented engine as a nucleus for its construction. The success of this engine is due to the combined efforts of Balzer and Manly.

23 May 1933—Affidavit sworn by Richard S. Newham before Robert T. Highfield, Notary Public, Washington, D.C.

I am a citizen of the United States and reside in the City of Washington, District of Columbia. I was educated at Cooper Union in the City of New York and in 1899 I was a resident of the City of New York, where I was working as an expert mechanic. I was employed in October 1899 by Mr. Stephen M. Balzer of the City of New York to work in his shop on the construction of certain working models of pneumatic tools and equipment that were exhibited in the Paris Exposition. While I was in the employ of said Balzer, Mr. Manly from the Smithsonian Institution at Washington, D.C. called upon Mr. Balzer to find out how work was progressing on an engine invented and designed by said Balzer which was under construction in the Balzer shop, on contract to said Institution, and a smaller replica of said engine, also for said Institution. Manly expressed himself as desirous of securing the services of competent mechanics to work on the construction of Professor Langley's Aerodrome in Washington; and he asked Mr. Balzer's assistance in securing such men. Early in 1900 Mr. Balzer sent two expert men, Messrs Philbrook and Wright, releasing them from employment in his shop to enter the employ of said Institution.

181

In the course of my work in Mr. Balzer's shop, I was called upon to assist in the testing of said large engine, in which capacity I became thoroughly familiar with its design and construction. While I was in the employ of said Balzer, I found him to be a mechanic of exceptional skill and a designer of unusual originality. I admired his ingenuity in the invention and reduction to practice of the radial four cycle internal combustion engine, as evidenced by the two said engines and a certain automobile he had constructed employing an engine of similar type, but water cooled. I have seen another of his automobiles of cruder construction along the same lines on exhibit in the museum of the said Institution, designated as a donation by said Balzer, and built in 1894.

In March, 1900 said Balzer released me from employment in his shop in order that I might enter the employ of the said Institution under the supervision of said Manly, who had been graduated as an engineer, but who was not a mechanic. Accordingly, I went to Washington in March 1900 to enter the employ of said Institution, and I remained there until May, 1904. In the shop of said Institution I worked on the construction of the Langley Aerodrome and on a small scale replica thereof.

About the middle of August, 1900 both of said engines were accepted and brought to Washington. The large engine had fallen somewhat short of its contracted 12 horsepower, and the small engine was incomplete to the extent that radiating fins had not been secured to the cylinders.

In Washington, slight modifications were made in the large Balzer engine in which work, I took an active part. This work, together with testing, occupied about a month in all, and consisted principally in holding the cylinder assembly stationary and rotating the crankshaft, whereas the engine had been originally designed for a stationary crankshaft with the radial cylinder assembly rotating as in the Gnome, Le-Rhone, Crossley, and other engines that became very popular during the World War. In the said testing in Washington, the said Balzer engine developed far in excess of its contracted power, but Mr. Manly decided that even more power would be required to fly the Aerodrome.

Accordingly Mr. Manly started work on a reconstruction of the large Balzer engine. I was detailed to construct various parts of this new engine. Balzer's main frame was used as a nucleus in this reconstructed engine, which had the same stroke but an enlarged bore,—the original Balzer engine having a four and three sixteenth inch bore and a five and a half inch stroke, while the engine as finally used in the Aerodrome has a five inch bore and a five and one half inch stroke. In this reconstruction, Balzer's radial disposition was used, and he shipped his special tools to said Institution to enable us to drill the new cylinder flanges to fit the original Balzer frame upon which the new engine was based. One of Balzer's supporting trusses was retained, and the other was replaced by a stouter copy of the original. Balzer's original cam and actuating mechanism and his original cam followers and cam follower supports were used. The reconstructed cylinders were built according to Balzer's unique method of shrinking steel sleeves over cast iron liners and then boring and finishing the assembled cylinders. The original Balzer engine was equipped when delivered by him with his unique carbureter comprising a sheet metal shell enclosing a mass of fragments of Tupelo wood into which the gasoline was fed. The engine as reconstructed under Manly's supervision, which was used in the Langley Aerodrome, was equipped with a copy of this carbureter built to a somewhat larger scale. The crank pin bearing on the original Balzer engine was found inadequate to handle the increased output of the reconstructed engine. This bearing comprised a segmental terminal on each connecting rod, each of which was retained by end rings, one on either end, which engaged all five of the segments. This bearing system was improved at the Smithsonian shop under Manly's supervision, by equipping one master rod with a bronze liner or bushing that bore directly on the crank pin, and upon the exterior of which the segments of each of the remaining four rods bore, the assembly being retained by the end rings. This bearing was found satisfactory. The make and break ignition system with which said original engine had been equipped by Balzer was not satisfactory, and Mr. Manly instructed us to make a copy of the De Dion jump-spark system that was installed on an engine he had purchased in France from Comte de Dion. This ignition system was successful.

I was well satisfied with my relations with Mr. Balzer while in his shop, and I was also well satisfied with my treatment under Mr. Manly, for whom I had a high regard. I consider the successful engine in the form in which it was finally used in the Aerodrome as the joint work of Balzer, who originated it and laid the foundations for it, and of Manly, who reconstructed and refined it.

Summary

Although neither Balzer nor Manly invented any of the engine's features, they were solely responsible for incorporating them in the design. The two most important of these were the radial disposition of an uneven number of cylinders (patented by Felix T. Millet of Beaumont, France—British patent number 5199 of 1889) and the master and link rod system (patented by George H. Corliss of Providence, Rhode Island —American patent number 17,423 of 1857).

A list of the important features, their advantages, and credit for their incorporation in the design follows:

1. Radial Configuration—This design was contributed by Balzer, and was the principal reason for the engine's light weight. The saving in weight was due to the short crankshaft and small "crankcase."

2. Odd Number of Cylinders—This was also contributed by Balzer. The odd number of cylinders permitted their firing in sequence for smoother engine operation.

3. Change for Aircooled Rotary Radial to Watercooled Static Radial—This modification was contributed by Manly with Balzer's approval. It was completed within a month and doubled the engine's horsepower. Manly made the change because of his mistaken theory that the rotary was only one half as efficient as the radial due to differences in their crank angles. The decision was fortuitous, however, because the valves, being freed of the centrifugal and inertial forces induced when the engine was run as a rotary, worked properly for the first time, and permitted the engine to develop its designed power. It was a mixed blessing, however, because a water cooling system had to be incorporated in the design which added to the engine's weight, bulk and complexity. Also the engine vibrated noticeably as a radial (rotaries have no absolute reciprocation and are therefore smoother) so flywheels had to be added with their weight penalty.

4. Master and Link Rod System—The Balzer-Manly rotary engine (first stage of development) was designed to develop 12 horsepower; however, soon after it was converted to a radial by Manly it produced

PROFESSOR LANGLEY'S MAGNIFICENT AERO ENGINE OF 1903

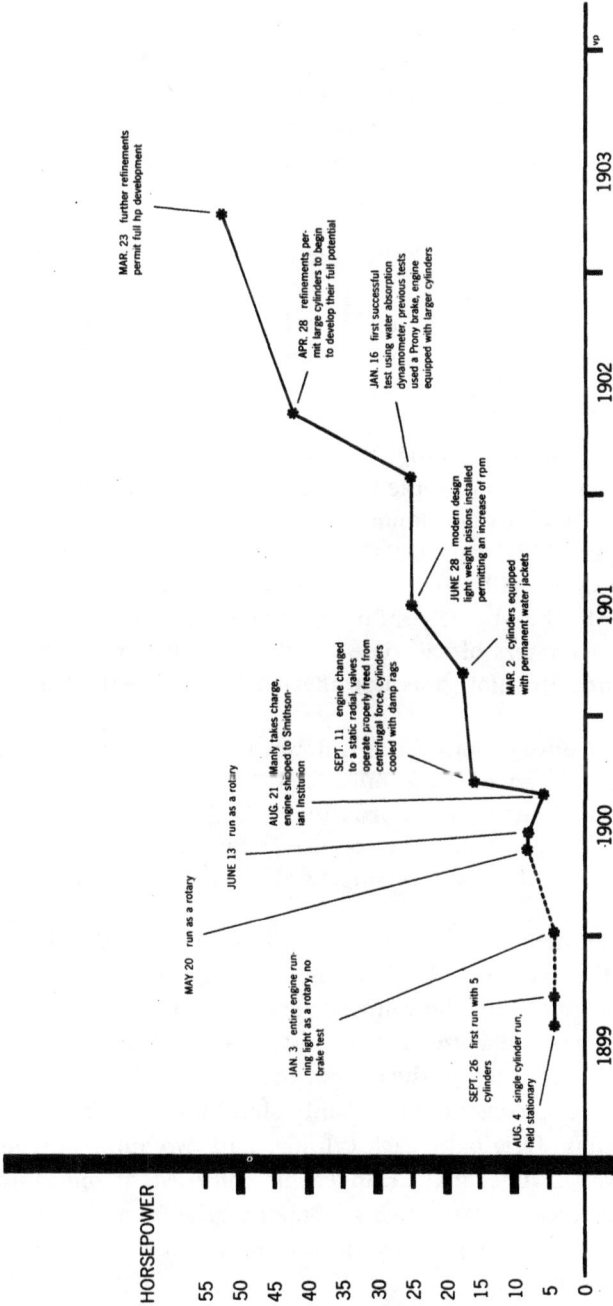

FIGURE 44.—Chart showing rise in horsepower of Balzer-Manly engine. Drawn by Harry T. Hart. (Smithsonian photo A4517–B.)

twice this power at which point the Balzer type of slipper bearings (connecting rods to crankshaft) proved inadequate. Manly solved the problem—lack of proper lubrication and sufficient bearing area—by devising a master and link rod system, and retaining the Balzer type of slipper bearings for the link rods. It is interesting to note that Manly's particular system was used in the Brownback "Tiger" engines as late as the 1930s. Almost all radial engines have had a form of the master and link rod system.

5. Ignition System—Balzer had originally decided to use the modern type of high tension or spark plug ignition system but changed his mind with Manly's approval, and produced instead the conventional (for the time) low tension or make and break ignition system. Later Manly changed this to the high tension system along the lines employed by the Museum's De Dion-Bouton engine.

In addition Manly placed the spark plug in the cylinder head which is a much more efficient arrangement than having the spark originate in a combustion chamber on the side of the cylinder as was the case in stage one of the engine's development.

6. Carbureter—This was the Balzer type consisting of a tank containing porous wooden balls into which fuel flowed and out of which vapors passed into the engine's induction system. It was superior to the automobile carbureters of the time for this special purpose because it was floatless and therefore was not affected by vibration or flight attitudes.

7. Cylinder Construction—Balzer's double-walled type of cylinder was used consisting of an outer seamless stell shell $\frac{1}{16}$ inch thick to provide strength, and an inner cast-iron liner also $\frac{1}{16}$ inch thick to provide a properly oiled bearing surface for the piston. This type of construction was much lighter than the single-walled cast-iron cylinder then in common use.

8. Piston Construction—Manly's design was based on the type of piston used in the Museum's De Dion-Bouton engine. It had thin walls and used a piston pin for the connecting rod bearing. Much weight was saved over the original Balzer type of pistons which had thick walls and a ball and socket bearing for the connecting rod.

9. Valve System Construction—Manly simplified and improved Balzer's valve system. Originally each cylinder had two automatic and one mechanical valve. The final arrangement consisted of one automatic and one mechanical valve. Much of Balzer's original actuating mechanism was retained, namely the two lobed cam together with cam followers and their supports.

186

Before Balzer started his controversy with the Smithsonian, he was not given official recognition on the exhibit's plaque. With the culmination of the controversy in 1933, the present exhibit label exemplifies this long overdue credit, which reads as follows:

BALZER-MANLY ENGINE
1901

The Langley Aerodrome of 1903 was powered by this engine, which developed 52.4 horsepower at 950 revolutions per minute. With 20 pounds of cooling water, batteries and accessories, it weighed 207.5 pounds, or 3.96 pounds per horsepower.

Constructed in the shops of the Smithsonian Institution by Charles M. Manly under the direction of Samuel P. Langley, it incorporates certain features of design from a rotary engine developed by Stephen M. Balzer. When bench-tested in 1902, the engine ran continuously for three 10-hour periods.

Epilogue

It has been the primary concern of this study to put in perspective the contributions of Stephen M. Balzer and Charles W. Manly in the development of Langley's aero engine, the most advanced of its kind in the world at the turn of the century. In the course of this survey, we have been able to answer some of the questions posed at the outset and to recognize that it was the combined genius of both men that made possible the creation of this engine.

It was in the attempt to recognize their contributions individually rather than jointly, that the inequities to their reputations were perpetrated. When the aviation industry finally grasped the significance of this engine's development and began copying the basic design on a large scale, it felt called upon to recognize the genius of at least one of the men responsible for its development. The engine had been so far in advance of the times that it had taken twenty years for it to be fully appreciated. Thus, it is greatly hoped that after 40 more years of controversy, this account has contributed in part to the full recognition of both Balzer's and Manly's participation in this pioneering project.

List of Names

ABBOT, CHARLES G., of Washington, D.C. At the turn of the century he was, "Aid Acting in Charge, Astrophysical Observatory" of the Smithsonian Institution. A prominent astrophysicist, he became the fifth Secretary of the Smithsonian Institution. Abbot, having worked under Langley, carried on his tradition as an astronomer, and has written several books on solar radiation.

AMES, JOSEPH S., of Baltimore, Maryland was a member of the National Advisory Committee for Aeronautics at its inception and rose to become its chairman. He wrote several books on aerodynamics, and became President of Johns Hopkins University.

BALLOU, JOHN McK., of Long Beach, California, is a consulting engineer. He was closely associated with Stephen M. Balzer for many years.

BALZER, STEPHEN M., of New York City was a master mechanic. He designed, built, and ran Langley's aero engine in its original configuration as an aircooled rotary radial.

BELL, ALEXANDER GRAHAM, of Washington, D. C., was a regent of the Smithsonian Institution. He is well known for his telephonic and phonographic apparatus inventions, and less well known for his experiments in heavier-than-air craft.

BOUTON, M. GEORGE, of Paris France, was the chief engineer of the De Dion-Bouton firm.

BRASHER, Dr. JOHN A., of Pittsburgh, Pennsylvania, designed and built telescopes. He worked with Langley at the Allegheny Observatory, and became its Acting Director. He then became Acting Chancellor of Western University.

VON BRAUN, WERNHER, of Washington, D. C., is a pioneer rocket expert. He was responsible for the development of the German V-2 long range missile of World War II. Shortly after the war he was invited to the United States to participate in its rocket development programs, and for several years was head of the George C. Marshall Space Flight Center, Huntsville, Alabama. He is presently Deputy Administrator for Planning, National Aeronautics and Space Administration. His abilities as a scientist, leader, and author have made him the world's most renowned living rocket and aerospace scientist.

BYRD, RICHARD E., of Winchester, Virginia, was a pioneer aviator, navigator, polar explorer, and author. He was the first to command and navigate flights over the north and south poles.

CORLISS, GEORGE H., of Providence, Rhode Island, patented the master and link rod design in 1857 (American patent number 17,423). This has been a feature of almost every successful radial engine built since the turn of the century.

CURTISS, GLENN H., of Hammondsport, New York. The most prominent pioneering American aviator after the Wright brothers. Like them he designed, built, and flew his own airplanes and engines.

DARCY. A Smithsonian carpenter.

DAVIS, Captain. A member of the Board of Ordnance and Fortification, Office of Secretary of War.

DE DION, COUNT ALBERT, of Paris, France. He was the administrator of the DeDion-Bouton firm.

DICKSON, T. C. Recorder for the Board of Ordnance and Fortification, Office of the Secretary of War; replaced Captain I. N. Lewis.

DRYDEN, Dr. HUGH L., of Washington, D. C. He was Director of the National Advisory Committee for Aeronautics and then became Deputy Director of the National Aeronautics and Space Administration, a position he held until his death.

EIFFEL, A. GUSTAVE, of Paris, France. Best known as the designer and builder of the Eiffel Tower and numerous bridges, he nevertheless spent more than a decade studying aerodynamics.

GREELY, Major General ADOLPHUS W., was Chief Signal Officer of the United States of America.

GODDARD, ROBERT H., of Worcester, Massachusetts, is known as the father of United States Rocketry. He built the first successful liquid-fueled rocket, and continued his developments to the extent that the Nazi government used his patents in its V–2 program, during World War II.

HADLEY, F. W. A clerk in Langley's office.

HEWITT, FRED. A machinist employed by Balzer to work on the Balzer-Manly engine, and then by Manly for the same purpose.

HODGES, F. W. A clerk in Langley's office.

HUNSAKER, Dr. JEROME C., of Boston, Massachusetts, is Professor Emeritus of Aeronautical Engineering, Massachusetts Institute of Technology. He was responsible for the design of various aircraft including the NC–4, first to cross the Atlantic Ocean.

KARR, W. W. Accountant of the Smithsonian Institution. During June 1905 it was ascertained that he had stolen $68,558.61 from the Institution over a 14-year period.

LANGLEY, SAMUEL P., of Washington, D. C., was the third Secretary of the Smithsonian Institution. Although a foremost astrophysicist and inventor of the balometer (a sensitive instrument for measuring the temperature of celestial bodies) he is best known for his experiments with heavier-than-air craft.

LAWRANCE, CHARLES L., of Long Island, New York. He was President of the Wright Aeronautical Corporation, manufacturers of the famous Wright J–5 "Whirlwind" which powered Lindbergh's "Spirit of St. Louis."

LECOEUR, of Paris, France. An engineer who was employed by the DeDion-Bouton Company.

LEWIS, I. N. Recorder for the Board of Ordnance and Fortification, Office of the Secretary of War.

LINDBERGH, CHARLES A., of Darien, Connecticut. Best known for his famous solo flight from New York to Paris in 1927, he is also well known as an author, aviation consultant, and conservationist.

LUDEWIG. A machinist who worked for Manly.

MACDONALD, GEORGE D. A machinist employed by Balzer to work on the Balzer-Manly engine, and then by Manly for the same purpose. The Wells diary entries misspell the name as "McDonald."

MANLY, BASIL, was a brother of Charles M. Manly.

MANLY, CHARLES M., of Washington, D. C., was Professor Langley's "Aide in Aerodromics." He built both of Langley's gasoline powered Aerodromes, and developed both of their engines.

MANLY, JOHN, was a brother of Charles M. Manly.

MAXIM, Sir HIRAM S., of London, England, was a famous expatriate American inventor. In 1894 his 3½ ton "lift test rig" flying machine "rose" from the ground.

MAYNARD, GEORGE C., of Washington, D. C., was Curator of the Department of Mechanical Technology, United States National Museum, Smithsonian Institution.

MILLET, FELIX T., of Beaumont, Texas, patented the radial disposition of an uneven number of cylinders in 1889 (British patent number 5199). This has been an important type of aero engine for more than 70 years.

MOLSON, E., was an entrepreneur interested in promoting Balzer's automobile business.

MOORE, EDGAR, was a friend of Dr. C. G. Abbot.

NEWHAM, RICHARD S. A machinist employed by Balzer to work on the Balzer–Manly engine, and then by Manly for the same purpose.

PHILBROOK, AUSTIN H. A machinist employed by Balzer to work on the Balzer-Manly engine, and then by Manly for the same purpose.

PIERCE. A machinist employed by the Smithsonian Institution.

PUGSLEY. Agent for Franklin Stock Cylinder Oil Company.

RATHBUN, R. Assistant Secretary of the Smithsonian Institution in charge of Office and Exchanges. He ran the Aerodromic projects whenever Langley was away.

REED, R. L., Foreman of Aerodromic Work. Worked on all of the Aerodromic projects. His specialty was carpentry.

RUSSELL. A machinist employed by Manly to work on the Balzer-Manly engine.

SCOTT, LLOYD N. Lawyer hired by Abbot, fifth Secretary of the Smithsonian Institution, to assist in settling the dispute between the Balzer and Manly partisans.

SHEPARD, ALAN B., JR., of Houston, Texas. First American astronaut in space.

SMITH, WILLIAM MCKAY, was an associate of Manly. Later he was placed in charge of the Switchboard Department of the Western Electric Company of New York City.

SPEIDEN, W. L. An independently employed draftsman who often did Aerodromic work for Langley and Manly.

STOUT, JOHN F. Balzer's Sales Agent.

STRATTON. [Not identified.]

THURSTON, R. H. Director of the Schools of Mechanical Engineering and of the Mechanic Arts, Sibley College, Cornell University. He had been a good friend of Langley for many years.

WALCOTT, CHARLES D. The fourth Secretary of the Smithsonian Institution, succeeding Langley.

WALTERS. An employee of Sir Hiram Maxim.

WATKINS, J. E. Curator of Minerals and Technology, Smithsonian Institution.

WEED, JOHN W. Balzer's bondsman.

WELLS, GEORGE B. Assistant to Manly for the Aerodromic projects. At Langley's request he kept a diary which is one of the most important sources of information about the Balzer-Manly engine.

WHEELER, CAPTAIN. A member of the Board of Ordnance and Fortification.

WILLENBROCK, BERTHOLD D. A bookkeeper of Balzer's.

WRIGHT, F. F. A machinist employed by Balzer to work on the Balzer-Manly engine, and then by Manly for the same purpose.

WRIGHT, WILBUR and ORVILLE, of Dayton, Ohio, were the first men to make powered, sustained, and controlled flights in an airplane, and land on ground as high as that from which they took off.

U.S. GOVERNMENT PRINTING OFFICE: 1971 O—382-902

www.ingramcontent.com/pod-product-compliance
Lightning Source LLC
Chambersburg PA
CBHW070445100426
42812CB00004B/1212